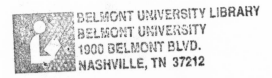

CLAREMONT READING
CONFERENCE
62ND YEARBOOK
1998

Reading, Writing, and Literacy:
Harmonizing Many Voices

Claremont
GRADUATE UNIVERSITY

READING, WRITING

AND LITERACY:

HARMONIZING MANY VOICES

SIXTY-SECOND YEARBOOK

OF THE

CLAREMONT READING CONFERENCE

Sponsored
by
Claremont Graduate University

Edited By

PHILIP H. DREYER

Continuing Conference Theme:

READING, THE PROCESS OF CREATING
MEANING FOR SENSED STIMULI

Price $20.00

Back issues of the Claremont Reading Conference are available
from two sources. Volumes still in print may be ordered from
the following address: Claremont Reading Conference
Yearbook, Harper 200, Claremont Graduate University,
Claremont, California 91711-6160. Write for information
concerning books in print and special price list. All past
Yearbooks are available through University Microfilms, 300
Zeeb Road, Ann Arbor, Michigan 48103.

Frank Smith's article, "Technology, Teaching and Literacy," is
copyrighted by Frank Smith, 1998.

ISBN #0-941742-18-0

Published by The Claremont Reading Conference
Institute for Developmental Studies
Claremont Graduate University
Claremont, California 91711-6160

ii

TABLE OF CONTENTS

ACKNOWLEDGMENTS

The 1998 Reading Conference was organized by a committee consisting of Abbie Prentice, Faith Bade, Nancy Brashear, Jane Carrigan, Thomas Caughron, Doty Hale, Sally Thomas, Carolyn Angus, Kay Grable, June Hetzel, Bruce Matsui, Carole Anne Weeks, DianaVander Wall, and Gordon Williamson. This group met regularly throughout the year and chose the conference theme as well as the keynote speakers. Each gave unselfishly of his or her experience and each deserves particular thanks. The entire conference was coordinated by Jane Carrigan who organized meetings, managed the mailing lists, corresponded with speakers, made the room arrangements, oversaw the publicity and the printing of programs, and solved the hundreds of problems that go with a conference of this size with good cheer and efficiency.

The preparation of this Yearbook was done by Teresa Wilborn and Ethel Rogers of Claremont Graduate University's Center for Educational Studies, while the cover design, layout, and printing were coordinated by Martha Estus of Claremont Graduate University's Public Affairs Office. Jane Carrigan organized the mailing and distribution of yearbooks.

Special thanks also go to the faculty in The Center for Educational Studies of Claremont Graduate University, especially Sally Thomas, Bruce Matsui, and David Drew whose creativity and support are essential to the continued success of the Conference.

Philip H. Dreyer
Reading Conference Director
Yearbook Editor

INTRODUCTION TO THE 62ND YEARBOOK

In past editions of this Yearbook I have discussed the ongoing controversy in the State of California about the best way to promote reading by children in the public schools. In 1995 California officially revised the language arts curriculum to require more emphasis upon the use of phonics instruction for all children in all primary schools. The result of this change has been to politicize the process of curriculum development in ways that few teachers or administrators have ever experienced. Curriculum materials in the language arts are "mandated" by State officials; materials sold by certain publishers are required at the exclusion of others; budgets and purchase orders are checked in some districts by citizen watchdog groups; and teachers are required to spend a specified number of minutes each day in the primary grades drilling students on the fundamentals of alphabet letter recognition, sight/sound correspondence, decoding skills, spelling, and phonemic awareness.

While no one argues the importance of all of these skills, controversy erupts when other aspects of the language arts curriculum are de-emphasized or ignored. For example, decoding and spelling of words is given high priority, but less time and effort are given to word comprehension and the meaning of sentences. Most important, the use of stories and other literary forms, such as picture books, children's literature, self-authored works, poetry, and drama, are de-emphasized in this new version of the "phonics only" curriculum.

Both proponents and opponents of these changes have tended to speak in extreme terms, claiming that their approach is not only best but also the only one supported by what they call "the research." While both sides are not above personal attacks against the other in any media forum they can command, each seeks rhetoric to claim the middle, more moderate ground. One side, for example, pushes phonics as the best way to "balance" the curriculum, while the other insists that whole language is "inclusive" of all methods, including phonics. The level of emotional involvement and animosity by both sides against the other is extraordinary, to the point where the heat of the argument overwhelms whatever light might emerge.

These political and educational debates would be more interesting and perhaps even useful if it weren't for the devastating effect they have on the morale and professional pride of classroom teachers. For the most part, classroom teachers have not been consulted about any of these curricular reforms, while their unions have opposed them. The basic trust in the competence of teachers and the faith that teachers know what they are doing and are acting in the best interests of their students has been eroded by a long series of negative stories in the media and negative presentations by politicians at all levels. Veteran teachers who have devoted their careers to making their classrooms exciting places for learning and who have successfully educated generations of children are now told what they can and cannot teach, what books they must use, and how many minutes of each day they must spend on certain activities. And young teachers, who look forward to expressing their creative energies by engaging children in exciting new lessons and activities, find themselves struggling to keep up with a bureaucratic regimen which stunts their professional growth and undermines their effectiveness. Few people who are involved in the reading curriculum controversy seem to care much about its effects on teachers; yet without the active participation and support of the teachers no curriculum reform can succeed. So it is important to build the morale of teachers and to provide them with the tools and support they need to work effectively with our children.

In this context the Claremont Reading Conference is a forum where teachers and educators who care about children and literacy come together to inspire and be inspired by each other. Our aim is to support teachers by encouraging them to share their best professional insights about what reading is and how they can improve their best classroom practices.

In doing this we begin with a clear point of view about what reading is—a view which was articulated many years ago by Peter Lincoln Spencer, a professor of education at Claremont Graduate University who defined reading as "making meaning from sensed stimuli." Whether it is words printed on a piece of paper, symbols on a computer screen, sounds expressed by voice or other instruments, or movements made by the body, we all create meaning from our experiences, and it is this process of the construction of meaning which we work to understand and encourage.

Teachers confronted with a classroom of eager children find this definition both challenging and inspiring. Challenging because it puts the emphasis upon what each child does in the face of an alphabet letter, a word, or a story and how he or she develops the confidence and self-discipline to understand what these symbols mean. Inspiring because it opens up the classroom to all forms of experience and the liberty of creative action which confirms both the child's and the teacher's individuality and dignity.

The reading curriculum controversy will probably not end soon. But we cannot wait for that resolution to help the teachers who give so much of themselves to help children learn to read and write. For the curriculum is not the political mandate or the books and materials in classrooms. It is the teacher and what she or he brings into the classroom each day that matters. Without a sense of trust in the teacher and the teacher's commitment and competence there will be no education, so it is imperative that we engage and inspire teachers as creative professionals.

These issues were discussed at the 65th Claremont Reading Conference held on the campuses of the Harvey Mudd College and Claremont Graduate University on March 20 and 21, 1998, and the papers in this Yearbook represent some of those ideas and discussions.

Philip H. Dreyer, Ph.D.
Reading Conference Director
Yearbook Editor

TECHNOLOGY, TEACHING
AND LITERACY*

Frank Smith

It is a long time since human beings lived in a state of nature. Technology and its products today almost totally and inescapably frame everyone's life. By technology I mean all the systems, institutions, and devices that fill our world (like money, the law, automobiles, and computers). Technology may have been invented or developed by human beings, but it doesn't have the interests of human beings at heart—or any other interests, for that matter.

Technology nonetheless makes demands on people, and makes use of them. We may feel we are in control of technology because as individuals we can employ it in convenient or useful ways, like our automobiles and our bankcards. But as a mass, human beings are victims of the technology they have themselves created. Automobiles may destroy our environment and the banking system our economies.

Technology dictates the shape of industry, transportation, the economy, communications, medicine, agriculture, art, entertainment, and innumerable other critical aspects of contemporary existence. When computers shut down, banks, stores, airlines and hospitals can't function. We are obviously reliant upon computers—and I don't remember anyone asking if we wanted our world to be that way.

Electronic technology is now flooding into schools. Many teachers love computers in the classroom for the interesting experiences and useful activities they make possible. But other teachers fear computers as intrusions that distract their students and usurp their authority. Which group is right?

Both are. Computers are useful tools that should not be disdained, but also instruments of control that should not be ignored. Every technology changes our lives, whether we want it to or not.

Humans and Technology in Harness

It is a mistake to believe that all the different kinds of technology that we have today are the products of a few exceptional individuals, without whose innovations the technology would not exist. Almost everyone is involved in the evolution of the technologies that fill our lives, and the technologies themselves determine how they are developed and used at least as much as people do. Humans and their technology are inseparable.

If Edison hadn't invented the telephone, someone else soon would have. And nothing would have come of the telephone unless people, in the mass, hadn't admitted it into their lives. The development of technology depends on untold multitudes of people for whom we don't even have a special name. We could call them *understanders*. These are the people who *understood*, or *realized* technological possibilities for extending their own powers, adopted them, and learned to live with them. Without innumerable people submitting themselves to technology, all inventions would die of neglect (which millions of inventions doubtless have done). We are all understanders, and all technology is a part of us, potentially at least. Take ships as an example.

No one person was responsible for inventing ships, or boats, or even canoes. Human beings didn't so much invent water transport as *realize* that things could float on water, perhaps when they idly threw a twig into a stream or observed a log floating by. This was something that might have occurred to anyone, anywhere, requiring not so much a creative or inquiring mind as a receptive one. Minds, and there must have been many, had to be open to the idea that things could float, and from that to the idea that objects and even human beings might be transported upon things that float, and eventually to the realization that things might be *made* that would float and carry objects and human beings, and that ways might be developed to propel these floating objects through water.

Every step along the way, something that existed suggested a further use or development. Fabricated objects shaped their own development, as individuals *realized* that a further modification or utilization "made sense." Each successive step led to the next, but there would have been no next step if the previous one had not been taken.

The relationship between human beings and their technologies has always been symbiotic. Technology guides human beings in its own creation, suggesting (and even dictating) the manner in which it should be employed, and indicating (and even demanding) the ways in which it might be further developed. In taking the first step in the development and use of any technology, human beings in effect get on a moving walkway on which they can only go forward.

Technologies are inevitable and irresistible, given the imaginative power of people; not just technologies in general, but the very technologies that we have today. If we had to start all over again, the human race would to a large extent recreate precisely the technologies we presently have (or have had in the past, or will have in the future)—the same general body of languages, the same systems of mathematics, the same kinds of engine, automobile, jet aircraft, and computer.

Technology is irresistible because people constantly strive to further their own powers. They exploit anything that enables them to see further, hear more acutely, communicate more distantly, travel faster, carry heavier loads, expand memory, write faster and more legibly, and think more effectively. As a species, we can no more give up possibilities extended by technology than we could contemplate cutting off our legs or putting out our eyes. No technology has ever been discarded unless a more efficient one superseded it. We do not reject technologies "for our own good." There is always someone to pick up where another person may have decided to leave off, or to opt out.

Technology is inevitable because it is always modified for maximum effectiveness and utility with the resources currently available—a technological survival of the fittest. The clipper ships of the nineteenth century were close to being the ultimate sailing machines, the most efficient vessels possible, given the materials that were available at the time. The passenger jet aircraft today is close to optimum levels of performance, given the current state of materials, power sources, and human tolerance for being packaged into small spaces. Modern aircraft will doubtless be superseded, but only by a more efficient technology when new resources (including finances and other technology) become available.

Internally-Rooted Technologies

Most technology is physically distinct from human beings. We can turn our backs on it even if we can never escape it. Automobiles, jet planes, banks and legal systems exist wholly outside the human body, though they intimately influence the way we habitually think and behave. In a sense, most technology surrounds and embraces us.

But a few technologies are substantially located *within* the human brain, and exert their influence directly on thought and behavior. A primary and most potent example is language. In one respect language is a technology much like any other—it can be used in a variety of ways to express thought, share feelings, communicate ideas, and so forth. Indeed, language is often referred to as a tool.

But language is supremely different from most other technologies in that it is profoundly rooted in the human brain. Only the superficial tip of language floats on the surface of the external world. The bulk and foundation of language lie deep in the brain. We can never use language—speak, hear, read, or write—without the involvement of our thoughts, emotions, values and experience. Language is a seamless extension of the human nervous system. (Other means of expression and discovery that share a similar special relationship with our mind are mathematics, music, and art.)

Language provides a key example of symbiotic evolution. It wasn't invented by a few gifted individuals, or planned and propagated by committees. Language sprang up across the globe at roughly the same epoch in human development, and in a very similar form. All the 10,000 languages in the world today share the same basic structures of syntax and vocabulary; only the sounds are different. This basic form of language could not have spread so rapidly from person to person around the world before there were "mass communications." It must have arisen spontaneously and independently in many places.

A crucial trigger for language, and for many other aspects of human intelligence and social behavior, must have been a development in the human capacity for imagination, the ability to reflect and to consider what might be or what might have been. Another vital factor, springing from the same source, was the increasing complication of human life as it organized itself into communities requiring planning and foresight.

Given both the possibility and a need for reflection, for *realization*, the growth of language would have been inevitable, a natural extension of the protean human capacity for communication, organization, and thought. Language would have begun, everywhere, with the realization, not the invention, of a single word (though it would have been a different word in different places). In every community, individuals (not one individual) would have realized that a particular sound implied a particular feeling—which the same involuntary grunt implied that someone was hungry, or fearful, or proposed a hunting expedition. And one realization led to the next, as it was progressively understood that other grunts could imply hunger yesterday and hunger tomorrow, hunger in oneself and hunger in others, the absence of hunger and ways in which hunger might be avoided. The grunts would become voluntary, purposeful, and systematic. Language wasn't in the grunts, it was in their interpretation.

One word led to another, and another. There would be no stopping the progression until language was capable of expressing every human concept, every possible human feeling and thought. Not only did language develop relatively rapidly, it was relatively quickly finished. All languages are intertranslatable, even "ancient" and "dead" languages like Latin and Greek. Anything that can be said in one language can be said in another, with technical terms and shades of meaning accommodated by circumlocutions.

Everything that human beings might ever want to say, or rather, be able to say, can be said by the language we have today. Even computer technology has come into our lives without the necessity to invent new words for new concepts. Contemporary words have been borrowed and adapted for electronic purposes (like *memory, surfing, network, web*), a few old or specialized words have been revived (like *icon, cursor,* and the word *computer* itself), and neologisms have been constructed from amalgams or acronyms of existing words (*keyboarding, bit, byte, RAM*). In fact, it is difficult to see how we might have or understand a totally new concept, if no words exist in which the new concept could be expressed.

It is as if language, as it became established in the minds of individuals in every society in the world, scoured out the human brain for all conceptual possibilities. We may never say everything that can be said with the language potential that exists today, but there are no hidden reserves of language that would enable us to say things that in principle we could not say today. It is much the same with music, where all possible musical tones have been developed, though the number of possible harmonies and melodies that can be constructed from these tones seems endless. Mathematics, on the other hand, (with the exception of the number system, which was fully established almost as soon as it was conceived of), seems endlessly capable of bursting out in new directions.

Learning and Education

Learning is not a technology, though teaching frequently is. The so-called learning programs and systems that abound in the commercial world, invading education, are in fact *teaching* technologies, and teaching and learning are by no means complementary. Learning is a natural and continual function of the human body, as instinctive and ceaseless as breathing. Learning is mental growth, and like physical growth it is inevitable given a healthy and nurturing environment. The tragedy for most human beings, perhaps for all of us some of the time, is not that we fail to learn what we might want to learn, but that we cannot help learning things that we would be better off not learning.

Learning, as I discuss at length in *The Book of Learning and Forgetting* (Smith, 1998), is a social activity. Once we rid ourselves of the notion that learning can only take place in schools, as a result of formal and systematic instruction, we can see that it is natural and continual. We become the kind of person we are able to *identify* with, whether in the "real world," or in books, and to a lesser extent in drama and movies, on television and the Internet.

What makes all this possible? Imagination. We would be unable to identify with anyone, and therefore unable to learn anything except basic and brutish habits, without the unique power of the human imagination. (And imagination, of course, is central in our symbiotic relationship with technology.)

The three keys to human learning, therefore, are (1) imagination, (2) identification, and (3) social interaction. Teaching—and education—can never be successful in the absence of any of these three key factors. Teaching—and education—can never be successful without relationships among *human beings*.

Teaching

"Natural" teachers (as opposed to technological ones) are individuals with whom learners can identify. Such teachers are not necessarily in schools. They are the people we would like to be like, in some ways at least, and who help and encourage us to be like them. They range from the influential if not always (to us) desirable friends that our children have in and out of school to the members of the formal and informal associations of people that we affiliate ourselves with throughout our lives.

Effective teachers, in schools and all other educational institutions, are those who bring their students into contact with individuals (including themselves) with whom the students can most profitably and productively identify. Such teachers enable education to fulfill the three essential roles I have outlined for it—fostering the imagination, encouraging rewarding personal identification, and promoting social interaction. In short, effective teachers create the possibilities for experience that make worthwhile human learning possible. They bring human beings together in ways that permit affiliation and bonding. Technology cannot do this. Identification with a computer is a pathological condition.

In business, the "bottom line" of concern is inevitably expected to be *profit*. But in education, the bottom line should always be *human beings*. A plaque on the desk of President Clinton was supposed to remind him "It's the economy, stupid!" A constant reminder to individuals at all levels of education might be: "It's human beings, stupid!"

Literacy

The assertion that human beings and their personal relationships are at the heart of learning—that human beings can only learn from the company they keep—often raises concern for students whose access to others is limited. What about those who can never hope to keep the company of artists, athletes, mathematicians, builders, designers, environmentalists, adventurers, and entrepreneurs, who have little access to exemplary parents, good citizens, political activists and other role models? How will they be able to learn what these individuals might be able to teach them?

There is one potent way in which every community and every actual or idealized person can be made accessible to everyone, no matter how poor, shy, or physically isolated. That way is through reading. Reading is the greatest technology ever devised for bringing human beings together. Language is an extension of the central nervous system, and written language is the route through which the human mind can be extended into infinite realms of possibility.

A reader can identify with any character in any book, story or article, whether "real" or fictitious (all characters are real in the reader's mind). No one can come between a reader and the character being read about. No one can say that a reader is not worthy of that character's company, or can't aspire to be like that character. Many people lead richly rewarding and often unsuspected second lives through their reading. Many people have become what they are—sailors, surgeons, teachers, and legislators— through inspirations and models whose acquaintance they made while reading. Reading is a uniquely powerful, private and subversive activity.

Of course, there are other technologies apart from reading through which we can encounter human beings, identify with them, and share their ideas and their feelings. We can do so through television, movies, videos, electronic games, and the Internet. But the terms of engagement are different.

The first major difference between literacy and electronic technology is in the degree of control. The authority of readers is immense. They can skip a passage, or reread it many times, just when they want, in the way they want. They can move with ease forward and backward through text and time. They can read fast or slowly. They can savor the sounds of individual words and the cadences of phrases, or ingest great gulps of meaning. They can reflect on arguments, compare alternative points of view, agree or disagree, and make mental and marginal notes in their own time. Film and television do not offer the same possibilities of self-directed involvement. It is true those computers may one day be as flexible and convenient as a book—but then the computer will *be* a book.

Being able to fast-forward or back on a screen is not the same as skipping paragraphs or pages. Slowing the action or freeze-framing is not the same as focusing on particular parts of a text. Watching images of human beings engage in a dispute is not the same as participating in an argument. I'm not denying the emotional and even intellectual power of film and video, nor their dramatic appeal and ability to stimulate the imagination, but they could never take the place of reading and print. They are different modes of expression, not substitutes. In fact, if film in all its manifest forms and technologies had been developed before anyone had thought of reading and writing, it would still have been necessary, and inevitable, for reading and writing to be developed.

The second major difference between written language and electronic technology lies in the degree of personal involvement they encompass. Reading, like language in general, is primarily an internal technology; it can never be a passive activity. Reading fires the imagination and commands identification because of the participation it demands from the reader. A reader gripped by a narrative is also controlled by the narrative—another instance of symbiosis. A story or report that holds our attention requires a contribution on our part—in terms of background knowledge, prediction, understanding of genre, scene setting, disambiguation, gap-filling and continuity—comparable with the contribution of the author (Smith, 1988, 1994). This is the reason our attention can be held by badly written novels with cardboard characters, ludicrous scenarios and flimsy motivations; good readers flatter poor writers.

The power of reading is acknowledged by the eagerness of some people to suppress books and other forms of writing to "protect" the young from the possibility of being influenced by them.

And finally, we also learn. Reading teaches itself; or rather the authors of what you read become the teachers of what they write (Meek, 1988). But we not only learn to read through reading, we can also—if we engage in an appropriate act of identification with the author—learn about writing, spelling, grammar, expression, comprehension, and reasoning. Only through reading can we practice critical thinking, experiencing how to follow and even refute a closely reasoned argument, to go beyond the sound bite. When we identify with authors and with characters in books, we can arm ourselves for many challenging aspects of life.

Hardly any of this can be accomplished with electronic technology, even that which appears to involve reading and writing, because the technology obscures the person and blocks the interpersonal relationship. Education is human beings, stupid! Electronic technology is heartless, mindless, and impersonal, with no direct access to the human brain. Computers aren't people.

Technology and Education

Electronic technology seems capable of extending all human capacities. It enables us to travel faster and further, extends our reach and our vision, permits us to make more complex calculations and to organize vast quantities of knowledge. It helps writers to write, builders to build, and musicians to compose. Technology is wonderful; I'm all for it, in daily life or in the classroom. But electronic technology also helps us, if we so desire, to extend control and surveillance over other people and to engage in all kinds of oppressive and manipulative activities.

All technology is double edged. The classroom equipment intended to help students achieve computer literacy, whatever that might be, may also make them susceptible to mindless "teacher-proof" instruction. The computer that helps students engage in music, art and writing can also be a teaching machine with as little educational value as an arcade game. The Internet opens up worlds of information, illustration, and interaction, but it can also allow perverse tentacles of the outside world to establish themselves in classrooms.

The computer is ubiquitous and seductive. It naturally appeals to many teachers, students and other creative people. But it is also irresistible to anyone dedicated to management systems, accountability, and the economic bottom line. To such people, computers are cheaper, more efficient and more reliable than humans. Computers never require holidays, benefits, or any kind of respect. Their efficiency resides not only in their fabled memories and speed of operation, but in their ability to organize anything that can be reduced to *data*. They are unparalleled in the establishment of records through questions, interrogations, censuses, information sharing, and (particularly in the case of education) tests.

Electronic technology is the inevitable next step in the systematization of education that began in the 1850s with the grouping of students on the basis of age and ability, facilitating instruction on a production line model, creating artificial competition, bogus success and failure, and ensuring that students are unable to help each other (Smith, 1998). There followed in rapid succession the wholesale adoption of experimental psychology's theory of learning, based on the memorization of nonsensical materials under artificial laboratory conditions, and the ever-growing practice of testing, adapted from dubious medical assessments for eugenic purposes and the wholesale mechanical categorization of individuals in the armed services. Outside authorities that were experts in just about any subject except teaching began to assert what teachers should do, and specialists in logistical approaches to the management of huge systems and enterprises designed objectives and procedures that teachers were expected to follow. In the process, human beings—as individuals and as communities—were lost sight of.

Mandated curriculums and the constant surveillance of teachers through test results would be impossible without computers. Computers can also administer and monitor instruction, broken down into data-sized scraps and dressed up as "fun." For anyone who believes that learning is a matter of systematic memorization, drills, exercises, effort, rewards and punishments, technology is more efficient than teachers in the classroom.

Common sense might say that computers could never take the place of human teachers, or of books. But in most political and administrative decision-making, common sense is seen as unreliable, emotional, and subjective. For those who don't trust common sense, the allure of computers lies precisely in their lack of emotion and subjectivity. A compassionate computer is an oxymoron.

Computers may seem expensive compared with the library books and the writing, music and art materials that they replace in schools. But they are infinitely cheaper than the teachers they displace. They have already pushed librarians out of many schools, claimed the salaries of innumerable support staff, and shut down "frills" ranging from art supplies to athletics equipment.

Teachers are the most expensive line item in any educational budget. And there is no shortage of claims that commercial instructional materials can take the place of teachers, or at least replace them with unskilled "aides." And there is no shortage of politicians and editorial writers who succumb to such blandishments. If teachers are found to be redundant in education, can school (and university) buildings be far behind? Instruction can be delivered wherever there is a television set—and is anywhere left in the world where there isn't one? Computers are already widely used to "deliver instruction," in so-called "distance learning," home schooling, and industrial training. In many colleges and universities possession of an electronic notepad is mandatory for students. School systems are rushing to link themselves to the "information highway" through "learning networks."

Computers can't take over the teacher's role, because computers aren't human, and learning only takes place through identification and interpersonal relations. Electronic technology can't take the place of books, because it doesn't facilitate the imaginative flow and personal identification that learning requires. None of these arguments, however, has any effect on people who believe the bottom line is economics.

And short of a revolution, which I think is unlikely to occur and even less likely to succeed, such attitudes will not be changed. After all, labor costs are a primary challenge to management experts. Human beings are being displaced where they were once considered essential. All around us we see the growth of tellerless banking, shopless shopping, driverless transportation, pilotless flight, and surgeonless surgery. Why should teacherless teaching be far behind?

Saying that education *needs* teachers won't protect them. People once argued that horses were essential for road and rail transport. We already hear that schools can't afford the teachers they have, that class sizes must grow, and that "interactive" technology can deliver personalized instruction.

Teachers are under pressure from all levels of government, from academics and self-proclaimed experts, and from vast commercial enterprises in the "communication" industry. Sometimes these groups work together, as they currently do in the passage of federal and state legislation mandating mechanical ways in which teachers should teach reading, language, or mathematics. But often the machinations of these pressure groups are unobtrusive and insidious, ranging from the silent lobbying of legislators to purchasing influence in schools through "gifts" of programs and equipment, with guarantees of "results."

Can electronic technology take the place of teachers, and of books? Never. Will electronic technology take the place of teachers, and of books? I'm not sure.

Living With Technology

It is unrealistic to believe that electronic technology can be kept under control in education, much less driven out. Trends over the past ten years show diminishing respect and support for teachers and growing faith in technology and centralized management systems. Computers could threaten both teaching and literacy, two fundamental sources of our growth as human beings. And there may be little that teachers, or anyone else, can do directly to delay the inrush of technology into their lives. But that does not mean that teachers need be helpless.

Technology may not be defeated, but we don't have to surrender to it. We can conspicuously uphold our own values, using technology where it is to our advantage, being wary of how it is used against us, and striving always to ensure that *our* bottom line is always human beings. Teachers and literacy must be protected.

The struggle in education is no different from that which must be fought in many aspects of national economies. We are constantly told that we can't afford the money that is spent, or should be spent, on health, welfare, working conditions, public safety, consumer protection, preserving the environment, and much else that is critical in our lives. We are barraged with the idea that any public good that does not meet the bottom line is unsustainable. We must always remember that the bottom line is human beings. We must learn to support and respect each other, preserving our own values while constantly exposing the dangers and threat of the opposing point of view.

The first step is to recognize where "efficiencies" supposed to benefit education are in fact methodologies of constraint and control. The second step is to raise awareness, in ourselves and others, of the struggle in which we are engaged. As Margaret Meek has recently declared, the primary act of literacy for teachers, students and parents must be to examine critically the mass of official documents and academic prose that claim to be advancing literacy (Meek, 1997). Who is writing the orders, planning the instruction, and setting the standards? What are their values and agendas?

The second step must be to display and assert our own values, to our opponents whenever possible, but constantly to our essential allies—other teachers, our students, their parents, and the public in general. Collaboration with those who want to regulate, standardize, monitor and depersonalize should only be done under protest. Acts of defiance— insisting that human beings must have priority over technology—should be overt where possible and subversive where necessary. Mutual support should be the lifeblood of the teaching profession. Teachers may on occasion need to "upgrade their skills" at workshops and conferences, but it is far more important for them to establish collegial relationships and show a common front.

We can't stop the advance of electronic technology—but this is not a message of hopelessness. We can't change the weather, but we can strive to maintain and advance what is important in our lives despite it. We can take advantage of the weather when it favors us and protect ourselves when it doesn't. And we can do the same with electronic technology. Many classrooms are secure enclaves of imagination, identification and personal relationships despite the storms that rage around them.

The idea must not be allowed to die that we live in a world of human beings, not in a world of machines, systems or lean budgets. Relationships among people constitute the heart of education, which must be kept beating no matter how heartless the environment in which we may be constrained to live, teach and learn.

References

Meek, M. (1988). "How Texts Teach What Readers Learn." In Martin Lightfoot and Nancy Martin (Eds.). *The Word For Teaching Is Learning: Essays For James Britton.* London: Heinemann
_____. (1997). "Rhetorics About Reading: Becoming Crystal Clear." *Changing English*, 4, 2, pp. 259-276.
Smith, F. (1988). *Joining The Literacy Club.* Portsmouth, NH: Heinemann.
_____. (1994). *Understanding Reading.* Mahwah, NJ: Erlbaum.
_____. (1998). *The Book of Learning and Forgetting.* NY: Teachers College Press.

CALIFORNIA EARLY LITERACY LEARNING AND READING RECOVERY: TWO INNOVATIVE PROGRAMS FOR TEACHING CHILDREN TO READ AND WRITE

Stanley L. Swartz

Introduction

In the past few years much has been made of problems facing the public schools. Of particular concern have been the reported difficulties that many children are having becoming literate (Education Commission of the States, 1995). These difficulties, whether real or imagined, have created a furor about the best way to teach children how to read and write. Many public schools have turned to outside experts to help them identify effective methods of literacy learning.

In California, a group of educators from public schools, universities, and foundations developed a partnership and completed an extensive review of available programs to address the needs of a large group of children considered at risk of reading failure. Three variables were important in the selection process; (1) only reading instruction methods with a strong research base would be considered, (2) the importance of early intervention would be paramount, and (3) the likelihood of general school reform through professional development must be evident. Two major initiatives have been undertaken because of this research: the development of a framework of early literacy activities in California Early Literacy Learning, and the implementation of Reading Recovery in California.

California Early Literacy Learning provides professional development in a basic system of classroom instruction designed to ensure early acquisition of literacy. Each child is provided a powerful learning experience in a classroom designed to accommodate multiple levels of experience and proficiency. Reading Recovery is provided as a safety net strategy for those children who need extra help in learning to

read. The successful implementation of this model requires a
commitment to professional development.

California Early Literacy Learning

    California Early Literacy Learning (Swartz & Shook, 1994; Swartz,
Shook, & Klein, 1998) is a staff development program designed to
support elementary teachers in their efforts to strengthen their teaching
of reading and writing. The California Early Literacy Learning (CELL)
training model is a peer coaching approach to helping teachers learn how
to use a framework of teaching activities effectively in their classrooms
and how to integrate the individual elements of this framework into an
overall system of classroom instruction. CELL is also used as a school
change program that supports team building and school restructuring.

    The CELL model stresses and encourages active participation from
children regardless of their current level of literacy acquisition. High
progress children are encouraged to continue their rapid growth while
low progress children are guided through the process of literacy
acquisition with continuous support. The opportunity to try new
learning in a risk free environment and practice new strategies
throughout the day is encouraged. This model trains teachers to use a
gradual decline of teacher support and a gradual increase in student
independence based on demonstrated student capability. This decrease
in teacher support is based on observations of individual child growth in
understanding the processes of literacy. The child's use of a variety of
problem-solving strategies is supported through good teacher decision-
making about ways to assist each child toward the goal of independence.
The elements of the CELL framework for instruction are designed to
help each child and the whole class move together toward that goal. The
framework has been designed to structure a classroom that uses literacy
activities throughout every school day. This model emphasizes that the
primary instructional role in the elementary grades is to teach reading
and writing.

    The balance of literacy activities used in the CELL framework is
designed as a system that provides maximum learning opportunity for all
children in primary classes. This intense focus on literacy acquisition
can be expected to help children in the short term to gain proficiency in
reading and writing and in the long term to learn in other subjects when

literacy is a requisite skill. Each day in the primary classroom would include shared, guided, and independent reading and interactive and independent writing, all organized into a flow of activity that keeps all children involved. This system allows the teacher to engage each child at their level and to provide experiences that advance their learning. Children making good process can be given time for independent work and for activities that are self-directed or peer facilitated. Children not making adequate progress will need more intensive assistance.

To ensure schoolwide support for CELL, a School-Based Planning Team (principal, reading specialist, special education teacher, and one teacher from each grade level), participates in a year long series of school change planning activities and training in the elements of the framework. The teachers from each team receive initial training in the teaching methodologies and begin implementation of this framework immediately after the first session. They receive feedback regarding their efforts at each subsequent session. This format allows a school to begin partial implementation of CELL and develop a resource for observation, demonstration, and support of the project.

In the second phase of the CELL project a Literacy Coordinator is trained to serve as a school-based staff developer who supports the implementation of the framework. The Literacy Coordinator continues to work half time as a classroom teacher and is released half time to support CELL implementation. This individual has no supervisory responsibility, but rather serves as a coach and mentor to colleagues on the instructional team. One of the major strengths of the CELL training model is the effectiveness of peer coaching. The direct support of a colleague has been found to be more effective in facilitating change than the more traditional model of evaluation and supervision. The Literacy Coordinators use their own classrooms to demonstrate for their colleagues.

The CELL model is designed to make elementary schools self-sustaining through training of Literacy Coordinators who can provide staff development and peer coaching to teachers in their own school. This capacity-building model has been found to support long term change in participating schools.

Key Elements of CELL

There are key elements in the California Early Literacy Learning model that are important to school restructuring and professional development.

CELL recognizes that the teaching of reading and writing is the foundation for all later academic achievement. Teachers are encouraged to teach subjects using the framework of literacy activities. This restructures how we teach children to read and write by providing massive opportunities to practice in classrooms that use literacy activities as the basis for all instruction.

CELL is a balanced reading program that combines skill development with literature and language-rich activities. Teaching methods that have substantial support in the research literature are used, and teaching methods are aligned within and across grade levels.

Diagnostic information to inform instruction and assessment data to ensure accountability is collected in all schools. Teachers are helped to improve their observation of children to inform instruction. CELL is a program of intensive professional development that also includes follow-up. A capacity building model that ensures long term support is used. CELL success is measured by student performance and has shown comparable success with English language learners. CELL also has the necessary attributes of an effective immersion program for English language learners.

California Early Literacy Learning Research

CELL research has focused on six major areas (Swartz, Shook & Klein, 1998):

1. *Overall text reading increases.* Text reading for focus children in kindergarten, and grades one and two were measured in a large, diverse school in northern California. Observation Survey (Clay, 1993) average score increases for Fall and Spring testing were strong in all three grades, kindergarten (non-reader - pre-primer), grade one (end of kindergarten - grade two), and grade two (grade one - grade four).

2. *Impact of teacher training.* Text reading levels for children in classes of trained teachers were compared to scores of children in classes where teachers received no training in a rural Native American school in Wyoming. Children in classes with trained teachers had significantly higher scores in each grade level than those children in classes where teachers received no training.

3. *CELL impact on Reading Recovery implementation.* Standardized test scores (Comprehensive Test of Basic Skills) were measured for children in grade one over a period of four years in a district with Reading Recovery implementation in years one, two and three and CELL School-Based Planning Team training in year four. Scores in total mathematics, total reading and total battery increased from a 22-31 national percentile range for Reading Recovery implementation to the 44-50-percentile range with the addition of CELL training.

4. *Effect of developing local capacity.* A study to assess the impact of training of a CELL staff developer was conducted over a three-year period. Significant increases in text reading scores were found in successive years from Reading Recovery training in year one, CELL School-Based Planning Team training in year 2, and Literacy Coordinator training in year three.

5. *Impact on special education referral.* Referrals to special education were tracked in a large, urban school district in southern California. In Title I schools with Reading Recovery referrals to special education were reduced by one percentage point over a three-year period. Schools with Reading Recovery and CELL implementation reduced two percentage points over the same period. A preliminary report of a study to track referrals to Reading Recovery in CELL schools is showing a similar reduction in referrals.

6. *Benefits of full CELL implementation.* A study that compared full CELL implementation (School-Based Planning Team and Literacy Coordinator training), partial CELL implementation (School-Based Planning Team training only), and CELL clone training (training similar to CELL training but with reduced levels of training) found a significant increase in reading scores for those children in schools with full CELL implementation.

Reading Recovery

Reading Recovery is an early intervention program designed by
Marie M. Clay (1979, 1985) to assist children in first grade who are
having difficulty learning to read and write. Children eligible for the
program are identified by their classroom teachers as the lowest in their
class in reading acquisition. Children who are not taking on reading and
writing through regular instruction receive a short-term, individually
designed program of instruction that allows them to succeed before they
enter a cycle of failure. Reading Recovery is designed to move children
in a short time from the bottom of their class to the average, where they
can profit from regular classroom instruction. The goal of Reading
Recovery is accelerated learning. Children are expected to make faster
than average progress so that they can catch up with other children in
their class.

Reading Recovery provides one-to-one tutoring, five days per week,
30 minutes a day, by a specially trained teacher. The daily lessons
during these 30 minute sessions consist of a variety of reading and
writing experiences that are designed to help children develop their own
effective strategies for literacy acquisition. Instruction continues until
children can read at or above the class average and can continue to learn
without later remedial help. Reading Recovery is supplemental to
classroom instruction and lasts an average of 12-20 weeks, at the end of
which children have developed a self-extending system that uses a
variety of strategies to read increasingly difficult text and to
independently write their own messages (Swartz & Klein, 1997).

Reading Recovery was designed to help otherwise successful
teachers acquire the necessary understandings and skills to assist
children who are at risk of failure in reading. Emphasis is placed on
training teachers working with the children at the beginning of their
literacy learning so that any misunderstandings or confusion that might
occur in the child's thinking could be addressed early to avoid the
habituation of a misplaced skill or strategy.

Teachers are trained to understand what a child may be thinking by
becoming highly effective observers of children. The systematic
observation that is key to Reading Recovery helps teachers learn to
watch a child's behaviors while reading and writing and informs the

teacher as to the probable processes the child is using or misusing as he reads or writes. The teacher can then guide the child to a more effective and more efficient strategy or skill.

Key Elements of Reading Recovery

Reading Recovery has a number of key elements that make the program an important opportunity to reform how we teach young children to read and write.

Reading Recovery is an early intervention program that supports early literacy. Reading Recovery focuses on early intervention, the advantages of which have been well documented. Beginning early, before problems begin, rather than on later remedial programs, has benefits to both individual student achievement as well as program cost effectiveness. Reading Recovery is designed to concentrate resources on first graders as they begin to read.

Reading Recovery also supports accelerated learning. Most remedial programs consider themselves successful even when only a small amount of progress is made. Unfortunately, children making only little progress will always be behind their class. Only acceleration can help a child catch up to the average of his peers and allow participation in the regular class program.

Reading Recovery serves the lowest achieving children. The lowest children in first grade, without exception, are selected to receive the program. None of the usual reasons used to explain non-achievement (e.g., likely referral to special education, lack of parental support) are used to exclude children from the program. Reading Recovery is effective with diverse populations. Data collected on program success from different geographical regions (throughout the United States, Australia, Canada, the United Kingdom, and New Zealand) and from various groups of children (those with ethnic, language, or economic differences) are comparable. Preliminary data from the more recently developed Descubriendo La Lectura/Reading Recovery in Spanish are also similar to children receiving the English program.

Children develop a self-extending system of learning to read and write. Children learn the skills to be independent learners who will just need the support of regular classroom instruction rather than remedial programs. Student outcomes are sustained over time. Research on students after program completion has demonstrated continued growth in reading and writing without continued Reading Recovery support or other specific interventions.

Reading Recovery teachers serve children as part of their training. Teachers in the program learn by doing and use the Reading Recovery lesson framework throughout their training year. Reading Recovery also provides continuous professional support for teachers. The continuing contact for trained teachers is provided as long as the teacher participates in Reading Recovery.

Unlike other teacher education programs that have little contact with students after the training period, Reading Recovery has ongoing in-service opportunities designed to maintain and improve teaching effectiveness. In addition, Reading Recovery teachers, staff developers, and university professors work with children daily.

Program success is directly tied to student performance. And by implication, success as a Reading Recovery teacher is related to student outcomes. Teachers are accountable for the amount of progress in reading and writing made by children in the program. Reading Recovery has been shown to be cost-effective because of its short-term nature. Comparable programs (e.g., Title 1, special education) are much more expensive because they are typically long-term. Reading Recovery has been found to be both less expensive and more effective (Swartz & Klein, 1994).

Research in Reading Recovery

Reading Recovery research has focused on five major areas:

1. *Increase in student achievement.* Studies have consistently shown that students served in Reading Recovery programs exhibit significant increases in reading and writing with a high percentage (80 percent and higher) of children performing at or above average (Pinnell, DeFord, & Lyons, 1988; Swartz, Shook, & Hoffman, 1993; Askew, Frasier, & Griffin, 1993; National Diffusion Network, 1996).

2. *Continued progress without tutorial.* The success of Reading Recovery in helping children develop a self-extending system of learning to read and write can be demonstrated with a comparison of program exit scores and end-of-year scores. Children served by Reading Recovery have consistently shown a continued increase in reading and writing achievement for the remainder of the school year (Swartz, Shook, & Hoffman, 1993; Swartz, Kelly, Klein, Neal, Schubert, Hoffman, & Shook, 1996).

3. *Longitudinal studies.* Reading Recovery has shown good maintenance of achievement for children who received a full program. Children followed into grade three (Pinnell, 1989) and grade four (Allen, Dorn, & Paynter, 1995) were found in the average range of their classes. One study in a large, urban district found slightly higher scores for children who had been provided a Reading Recovery program (Griese, 1995).

4. *English language learners.* Reading Recovery has been reconstructed in Spanish as Descubriendo La Lectura (Escamilla, 1987). Similar results have been shown in a comparison of children who received the Spanish version and the English version (Escamilla, 1994) and there was no significant difference in a study that compared children who where English speaking and received the English program, children who were Spanish speaking and received the Spanish program, and children who were Spanish speaking and received the English program (Kelly, Gomez-Valdez, Neal, & Klein, 1995). This last study suggests the possible use of Reading Recovery as a method of English instruction.

5. *Cost effectiveness.* Because programs of one-to-one tutoring are considered expensive, studies have been done to evaluate the effect of Reading Recovery on grade retention rates and special education referrals. Studies have found a reduced rate of referral to classes for learning disability specifically (Lyons, 1997) and special education generally (Colton School District, 1996). The cost savings of not placing a child in special education are considerable. Studies of overall comparison of Reading Recovery and grade retention, placement in a remedial reading program, and special education placement found Reading Recovery to be the most cost effective because of its short duration (Dyer, 1992; Swartz, 1992).

Conclusion

California Early Literacy Learning and Reading Recovery are two programs that can be used to support school restructuring efforts. CELL provides the opportunity for team building at the school site and a format for the planning activities necessary to the school change process. CELL also provides intensive professional development to help teachers improve their teaching of reading and writing. CELL has a primary focus of ensuring that children in the elementary grades have access to good first teaching. It is through this kind of a powerful beginning in school that fewer children will need later remedial or special education.

CELL requires a schoolwide commitment to change in teaching methodology. Teaching is aligned within and across grades with massive opportunities provided for children to practice their reading and writing skills. Methods of assessment that help monitor children's progress and inform teaching are used in addition to the usual methods of assessment used for accountability. CELL research has consistently shown significant gains in reading and writing. Studies have also demonstrated reduced referrals to special education and the benefits of schoolwide professional development and the use of a capacity building model.

Even with the good first teaching provided by CELL, a small number of children would still need extra help. Reading Recovery is a proven program of early intervention that provides a tutorial that accelerates the learning of children having difficulty. Though Reading Recovery is one-to-one program, it has been shown to be cost effective because of its short-term duration. Most children who have received Reading Recovery achieve in the average range and do not need additional support other than the regular classroom program.

Reading Recovery has been found to be a primary impetus for change in many schools participating in the program. Though logic would suggest that a schoolwide program like CELL would be the first step in the change process, the unexpected growth of many at risk children in the Reading Recovery program has been a powerful demonstration of what might be accomplished with school restructuring and different teaching methods.

Both CELL and Reading Recovery are programs that provide professional development for teachers. Both believe that effective school change and achievement gains for children are only possible with increased support and training for teachers. Teachers who can make good decisions about what children need, teachers who can select materials and plan good instruction, and teachers who are supported in their work are what is best for children.

CELL and Reading Recovery have the shared philosophy that all children are capable of becoming readers and writers. Both also support the ideas that children who experience difficulty in the process of learning to read and write do so primarily because of the teaching methods that are used. Reading Recovery and CELL also share a theoretical perspective that is constructivist in nature. From this perspective it is believed that working from what children know and providing teacher assisted scaffolding, children at all ages are capable of rapid growth in their learning. CELL for classroom instruction and Reading Recovery as a safety net combine programs that are highly compatible and designed to complement one another. These two programs have been found to be powerful agents for school change.

References

Allen, A., Dorn, L., and Paynter, S. (1995). "Are the Gains Made by Reading Recovery Students Sustained Over Time?" *Reading Recovery of Arkansas Newsletter*, 1(2), p. 7.

Askew, B., Frasier, D., and Griffin, M. (1993). *Reading Recovery Report 1992-93* (Tech. report, No. 4). Denton, TX: Texas Woman's University.

Clay, M. M. (1979, 1985). *The Early Detection of Reading Difficulties.* Auckland, New Zealand: Heinemann.

_____. (1993). *The Observation Survey.* Portsmouth, NH: Heinemann.

Dyer, P. (1992). "Reading Recovery: A Cost-Effectiveness and Education Outcomes Analysis." *Spectrum: Journal of Research in Education*, 10(1), pp. 110-119.

Escamilla, K. (1987). *Descubriendo La Lectura: An Application of Reading Recovery in Spanish.* Washington, DC: Office of Education Research and Improvement.

_____. (1994). "Descubriendo La Lectura: An Early Intervention Literacy Program in Spanish." *Literacy, Teaching and Learning*, 1(1), pp. 57-70.

Griese, D. H. (1995). *Evaluation of the Reading Recovery Program in the Long Beach Unified School District, Year 4 - 1994-95*. Long Beach, CA: Office of the Assistant Superintendent.

Kelly, P., Gomez-Valdez, C., Neal, J., and Klein, A. F. (1995). Progress of First and Second Language Learners in an Early Intervention Program. Paper presented at the American Education Research Association, San Francisco, CA.

National Diffusion Network. (1996). *1995-96 Discontinuation Data* (Research Report). Columbus, OH: Reading Recovery National Data Evaluation Center.

Pinnell, G. S., DeFord, D. E., and Lyons, C. A. (1988). *Reading Recovery: Early Intervention for At-Risk First Graders*. Arlington, VA: Educational Research Service.

Swartz, S. L., and Klein, A. F. (1994). "Reading Recovery: An Overview." *Literacy, Teaching and Learning*, 1(1), pp. 3-7.

Swartz, S. L. (1992). *Cost Comparison of Selected Intervention Programs in California*. San Bernardino, CA: California State University.

_____, Kelly, P., Klein, A. F., Neal, J., Schubert, B., Hoffman, B., and Shook, R. E. (1996). *Reading Recovery in California. 1995-96 Site Report*. San Bernardino, CA: California State University.

_____, and Klein, A. F. (1997). *Research in Reading Recovery*. Portsmouth, NH: Heinemann.

_____, Shook, R. E., and Hoffman, B. M. (1993). *Reading Recovery in California. 1993-94 Site Report*. San Bernardino, CA: California State University.

_____, and Shook, R. E. 1994. *California Early Literacy Learning*. (Technical Report). San Bernardino: California State University.

_____, Shook, R. E., and Klein, A. F. (1998). *California Early Literacy Learning*. (Technical Report). Redlands, CA: Foundation for California Early Literacy Learning.

CONSTRUCTING MEANING: NATURAL STAGES OR RIGID CURRICULUM?

Sharon Zinke

Rather than merely swinging to the right, our familiar pendulum is crashing into and through the wall of educational reform in our state. California appears to be suffering from a well-orchestrated push in the direction of skills-dominated reading instruction. In my role as a thirty-year veteran of teaching language arts, I must admit this has come as a surprise to me. The readings I have enjoyed over the past twenty years had convinced me, in my naivete, that the pendulum might have stopped in its tracks. We now know, with clear and growing evidence, that children demand, benefit from, and deserve learning that is meaningful to them, and that the children themselves, rather than a predetermined, contrived curriculum, must be most central to teaching and learning (Smith, 1986; Goodman, 1987; Holdaway, 1979; Weaver, 1994; Cambourne, 1988; Elley, 1992). But in spite of this flood of rich ethnographic classroom research that gives us such insight into what really goes on when children learn to read, we seem to be caught in a giant, stifling undercurrent, what Frank Smith calls the "official theory of learning," (Smith, 1998) that continues to define reading as separate, testable bits that must now be fed to our youngsters in a rigid sequence with a sizable pile of decodable books.

In the midst of the current political firestorms that appear to be spreading across the nation (Goodman, 1998; Taylor, 1998) and around the globe, a world truth has become clear to me. The idea was ignited when I read and reread sections of Constance Weaver's *Reading Process and Practice* (1994), and my own rich experiences with young children have brought focus to my study, fanning the flames. Children are individual human beings with individual needs, and must be honored and respected as individuals as they embark on their personal roads to literacy. Those of us who are privileged to be their mentors, whether we are parents or teachers, must take care not to hinder their progress by inflicting curriculum upon them that has its own sequence and content, as if all children need exactly the same interventions at the same time and in exactly the same way.

When conditions that support literacy (Cambourne, 1988) are present and addressed, my students move naturally through parallel stages of reading and spelling (Weaver, 1994) toward a personal command of written language. One might ask how so many of us learned to read without tremendous effort, when we were subjected to structured, pre-devised instructional programs as young learners. I believe that children with literacy and supportive adult-child interaction in their homes will move forward in their development, and through the same natural stages, in spite of the restrictive programs that they experience in school. The brain is capable of adapting to many varieties of instruction, the success of which is driven by the needs of children to make sense of their environment. Beyond this, however, we would do well to question the implications of one approach over another in nurturing children's overall development (Coles, 1998).

As I observe my students and their diverse range of strengths and needs, I wonder how a teacher could, in good conscience, require her first-grade students to begin the school year reading, or attempting to read, only books with a high percentage of words that correspond to phonic elements that have been taught in a publisher's predetermined sequence—so-called "decodable books." Aside from the obvious problems associated with forcing students to focus almost exclusively on the graphophonemic cueing system to the exclusion of meaning-based cueing systems, what about the students who are not yet ready to focus on and be held accountable for the intricacies of print? What about first-graders who are early emergent readers? Are we going to force them to repeat their humbling experiences sounding out the words in contrived short-vowel booklets until they finally master them? How will they feel about reading when their most vulnerable and impressionable first days have been spent holding hands with failure and comparing themselves with peers who seem to be leaving them in the dust?

I have found that it is easier to answer the questions that come up in these highly politicized times when the issues are viewed through a lens that acknowledges the diversity and range of children's early development. It is easy for me to know what to do for each of my students when I can identify their approximate stage of development (see

Figure 1). Children move forward through these stages, or phases,
fluidly and very individually toward a mastery of strategies that allow
them to interact with print in a powerful way.

Figure 1
Parallel Stages of Reading and Spelling

READING	SPELLING

Schema	**Prephonemic**
(no phonetic consciousness)	
• awareness of story comes from picture • may know printed word tells story	• journal entry is a picture • may attempt to communicate using scribbles, letter-like symbols, or actual letters
Semantic/Syntactic	**Phonemic/Letter-name**
(knowledge of letter/sound correspondence increasing)	
• beginning to match oral rendition with printed language • starts with tracking left to right building to one-to-one correspondence	• words begin to be represented by 1-2 letters, words may be left out • finally there will be 1 letter for eac sound the child pronounces
Graphophonemic	**Transitional**
• almost an over-attentiveness to letter-sound correspondence • will read word by word • will begin to self-correct using letter-sound correspondence	• some conventional spelling • will over-generalize spelling patte • becoming aware of exceptions to orthographic rules
Simultaneous Use	**Conventional**
• uses all three cueing systems to make sense of print	• when guessing, aware that it is a guess • able to recognize misspellings during editing stage

Source: Adapted from Constance Weaver, *Reading Process and Practice*, 1994
(in collaboration with Jennifer Jones-Martinez).

Deron was a second-grade student who was found to be eligible for special education in my elementary school. During first grade he did not speak to his teachers or even to his friends, except in one or two-word phrases. But he was lucky enough to have a teacher who understands the reading process and who was able to recognize that Deron was in the schema stage. He was reading lots of books, focusing on the pictures. He enjoyed reading, and his teacher encouraged him, giving him the opportunity to develop his sense of story, his language, and his love of books. Deron's spelling was at the prephonemic stage. His writing was fluent; he felt comfortable communicating with letter strings and pictures.

Deron's teacher knew that he had grasped the idea that the print somehow goes with the story or song and that he was just beginning to notice words and to make distinctions between them. She would not consider subjecting Deron or any of his classmates who were at this stage to a series of decodable books. Instead she gave them lots of meaningful experiences with stories and songs and poems. She helped them notice the letters in their own and their friends' names, and focus on letters and sounds in daily collaborative and interactive writing activities. They had daily experiences with shared reading and enjoyed reading predictable books with partners, focusing on the pictures. The teacher could see that these students were just beginning to make letter-sound connections in their writing, which signals a shift to the semantic/syntactic stage in reading. Her students often chose to read and write during free choice activities; even at this early stage, they saw themselves as readers and writers.

Seandae had made some connections between story and print and she knew how to point to the words on the pocket chart and in predictable books that were kept within reach on the table she shared with several other students in her classroom. As with Deron, her reading sounded fluent because she did not focus on particular letters within the words on the page; instead, she relied heavily on her excellent memory. Since she did not yet use letter-sound correspondence in her reading, she happily flew over the words and phrases, unconcerned that what she was reading did not quite match with the print. At the semantic/syntactic stage, she was over-relying on meaning and syntax to make sense of the books she read. She understood the concept of separate words in print and could follow along during shared reading. She knew some of the letters and the sounds that they make, but if you asked her to find a particular word in the passage that was just read, she would have to start at the beginning, pointing to each memorized word, in order to point it out.

But her writing! That's where you could see Seandae's blossoming use of letter-sound correspondence. At the phonemic/letter-name stage, she was using her budding phonetic understandings to get her thoughts down on paper. She, too, was fortunate enough to have a teacher who encouraged her phonetic or invented spelling. This teacher knew that giving her students the chance to learn from making their own spelling generalizations, combined with exposure to more and more books and print, would lead to a powerful command of conventional spelling. And she knew that her students would have a good chance of finding their own voices in their writing because of the green-light signal from their teacher. Seandae felt safe in her classroom to explore written language and to express herself in writing.

Aside from their own ingenuity, what is it that propels children into the graphophonemic stage of reading? Is it a series of rigid, scripted lessons from a teacher's manual and a set of decodable books that must be "read" in a sequence, designed by a group of adults who have never even seen these children? Or is it good teaching by teachers who have observed their students, who know which students are ready to focus on letter-sound correspondence and have a solid foundation of reading to construct meaning; teachers who know how to suggest appropriate books to their students and how to intervene in a way that supports a balanced use of cueing systems?

Children who have reached the graphophonemic stage are ready to use what they have learned from their independent writing, from shared reading and writing experiences, and from their own observation of print in its many forms, to focus on letter-sound correspondence in their reading. When they reach this stage, they are often so focused on the phonics that they temporarily lose the carefree fluency that they enjoyed at earlier stages. They begin to trip over words, repeat themselves, and reread portions of a line, in an attempt to self-correct and read more accurately. This choppy reading or slowing down is a natural part of a process that will lead to a much smoother self-monitoring during reading if children have had the opportunity to move through natural stages, reading books with natural language, from the beginning.

The graphophonemic stage of reading is the only stage in which a child might find a somewhat interesting distraction in a small pile of decodable books. For my students, however, the fascination is short-lived. Because they have enjoyed a steady stream of fun, predictable books and high-quality literature from the first moment they entered my classroom, it does not take them long to make the pronouncement of an expert: "These are not stories!" or "These books don't make any sense!" With that, they are pushed to the side. This disdain for decodable books is not a problem for me because, as these children's teacher, I am interested in helping them move forward to a final stage: simultaneous use.

A confident, self-monitoring reader uses all three cueing systems (semantic, syntactic, and graphophonemic) in an integrated way. Why would I want my students to practice using only one cueing system, the visual (and its link to the oral: that is, letter-sound correspondence), when what they need is a balanced control of multiple cueing systems? Instead of the unnatural language of decodable books, I want my students to run into words that their self-monitoring strategies will help them figure out. How are they going to learn to use all of the valuable information that is available to them—schematic, pragmatic, syntactic, visual, contextual—unless they have stories and poems and factual books that inspire them to problem-solve their way to understanding? I want my students to construct meaning for themselves and to discover the joy in it.

In the midst of a continuous flooding of California county offices and school district offices with reams of articles filled with questionable assertions regarding reading "research," we have a growing wealth of published confirmation that there is, in fact, no research that supports the use of decodable books over predictable books for beginning readers (Allington, 1997; Taylor, 1998).

Rather than mandating "teacher-proof" instructional materials for teachers, and restrictive, prescriptive phonics-driven books for first-graders, I suggest that we fill our poverty-stricken libraries (McQuillan, 1998) and our classrooms with books that will entice our fledgling readers. Let us provide staff development that supports teachers in their understanding of the reading process. When teachers who have this understanding are free to observe their students' individual literacy development, rather than spending hours each day subjecting their students to sequential, scripted materials, they will be in possession of information that is critical to providing the particular support and instruction that is needed for each child to move forward.

When I take my child to the dentist, I expect that the dentist will offer only the treatment that my child needs at that moment in time. I trust the dentist to take a close look at my child's teeth, and to know what particular treatment would benefit my child. I would hope that the parents of students in California schools would ask for no less.

References

Allington, R. L., and Woodside-Jiron, H. (1997). *Adequacy of a Program of Research and of a "Research Synthesis" in Shaping Educational Policy.* Albany, NY: National Research Center on English Learning & Achievement.

Cambourne, B. (1988). *The Whole Story.* Ashton, Scholastic.

Coles, G. (1998). *Reading Lessons.* Farrar, Straus & Girous.

Elley, W. B. (1992). *How in the World Do Students Read?* The IEA Study of Reading Literacy. The Hague, Netherlands: International Associations for the Evaluation of Educational Achievement.

Goodman, K. S. (1998). *In Defense of Good Teaching: What Teachers Need to Know About the Reading Wars.* York, ME: Stenhouse.

Goodman, Y., Watson, D., and Burke, C. (1987). *Reading Miscue Inventory.* Portsmouth, NH: Heinemann.

Holdaway, D. (1979). *The Foundations of Literacy.* Portsmouth, NH: Heinemann.

McQuillan, J. (1998). *The Literacy Crisis: False Claims, Real Solutions.* Portsmouth, NH: Heinemann.

Smith, F. (1986). *Understanding Reading.* Hillsdale, NJ: Lawrence Erlbaum Associates.

_____. (1998). *The Book of Learning and Forgetting.* Teachers College, Columbia University: Teachers College Press.

Taylor, D. (1998). *Beginning Reading and the Spin Doctors of Science.* Urbana, IL: NCTE.

Weaver, C. (1994). *Reading Process and Practice: From Socio-Psycholinguistics to Whole Language.* Portsmouth, NH: Heinemann.

HARMONIZING MANY VOICES: TALKING, LISTENING, READING AND WRITING

Lil Thompson

I usually begin with a poem. This one is by Elizabeth Farrer.

Etcetera

In the beginning someone gave us two hands, ten
fingers, two ears, one mouth, two eyes and a few million
nerve ends.
We learned to handle wood, wool, stone, etcetera
Hear music, laughter, bird song, Beatles, etcetera
See skies, blue, vast, shining, etcetera
To love, hate, want, need, cry, etcetera
So now we sit on wooden boxes at wooden boxes
And wait for the OK list of rules to be handed out
By someone, who some years ago,
Went through the same process.
If you put a coin in a slot machine
And pull the handle, you get an answer.
The answer you put in in the first place
It's a wonderful thing,
This Education.

Cynical, yes, but there are some truths there. When I received the
theme for the 1998 Reading Conference, I was delighted that I could
speak to it with real feeling. Twenty-five years before I had been invited
by Professor Malcolm Douglass to speak at the conference. He had
visited my school and had seen at first hand how I tried to link the very
important areas of literacy. My children could listen, talk, write, and
read for I could not separate these. Remembering my own childhood
inspired me to create a very different environment for my children. I had
had to sit up, hands behind my back and was only allowed to speak when
I was spoken to. There were times when, overcome with frustration, I
would say something in a whisper. I was convinced that my teacher not

only had "all seeing eyes" but "all hearing ears" as big as elephants as well. I would have to stand in the corner for talking. I wanted to share all the wonderful experiences I was having as I grew up; but that was not allowed. I thought that everybody would want to know that my pet rabbit had died and I wanted them all to come to the funeral. There was no sympathetic teacher to appreciate why my work was "poor" that day because I was emotionally disturbed. To be able to talk about it would have been such help.

Prof. Malcolm Douglass allowed me to talk about my educational philosophy, and I realize twenty-five years later that I got a standing ovation speaking to the same 1998 theme, only then I called it "Looking at Language." The development of language is all-important, and to encourage children to talk and listen was an excellent foundation for writing and reading. Even in those early days, I did not know which came first—writing or reading. I realized that young children would read their "scribble" to me. They could "read" pictures to me from the books I shared with them, and I knew that this was a very important stepping stone. I have stressed many times that as teachers, we must really know children—they are the materials we work with. Each child is unique. In forty years I never had two who were alike. I had to have a curriculum for every child. For all of them the important area was language development, harmonizing the many voices of literacy, listening, talking, writing, and reading.

The English Times newspaper stated "Learning to talk is the most difficult intellectual task, and on a child's verbal capacity gained early in life, depends much of its future development." The Plowden Report, which looked at child development in depth, told us that "Language is central to the whole process of education." Pestalozzi stated that "the child must be taught to talk before he can reasonably be taught to read. He must be brought to a high degree of knowledge, both of things and of words before it is reasonable to teach him to read or spell. It is good to make a child read and write, but it is still better to make him think."

I could quote many such statements from researchers, but as a teacher I know from experience that the child who comes into school with a good language foundation is the one who scores academically every time. As a young teacher the children I taught were not distracted by television and computer games. As early as 1908 Edmund Huey told us that "on the parent's knee, he comes to feel and say the right parts of the story or rhymes; his eyes and fingers travel over the printed lines." The *British Language for Life* said much the same thing a few years ago, "Place the child on your knee...and read to it." Dr. Maria Kelmer Pringle, in her ten suggestions for childcare, stated, "Bathe your child in language from birth onwards, it enriches his growing mind." I think I could use up my four thousand words by quoting all that has ever been said about the importance of language development. Having studied children from birth onwards I have marveled how they achieve mastery over grammar and vocabulary. They follow rules they do not know exist. By age three they can put words into a sentence. Nobody says to the three year old that to make the plural of a noun you add an "s"—but he does it, even adding a "s" to sheep—so that he has two sheeps! Nobody tells that same child that to make the past tense of a verb you add "ed"—but he will tell you "My Dad digged the garden" and "a bird flied over." Instinctively children follow grammatical rules they do not know exist, which is the miracle, and we wonder how that same child can add twenty new words each day without having a "word" lesson from anybody. It makes you wonder when twenty spellings are given and cannot be remembered where we are going wrong! Chomsby in 1965 started from the premise that children, far from being taught language, are innately "constructors who acquire language by discovering rules through problem solving and who make creative use of the rules to generate their own sentences."

There are 174 million adults in the USA. Over one third are unable to take advantage of the opportunities of American society. We still do not know, in spite of much research, how children learn to read or write or use language forms. To improve the mind, to enlarge the vision and to implant a sense of individual importance—these are the proper ends of education. Yet there is a paradox here for none of these things can really be taught. One of the complex tasks of education is to liberate and stimulate the unused or unrealized faculties of imagination and thought. My job as a teacher is to strengthen rather than fill the mind of the young child. We know that learning is continuous, spontaneous and effortless, requiring no particular attention, conscious motivation or specific reinforcement. Learning occurs in all kinds of situations and is not subject to forgetting. This is social rather than solitary. We learn from the company we keep, not from memorization—but growth. Learning through friends is effortless, unconscious and continuous throughout life. Social interaction brings about the growth of learning.

How do we put "language" into practice? How do we harmonize the many voices of literacy? We talk and listen to the child. The child who is read to at an early age is advantaged. Teachers should read to their children every day. Her role is critical, and interesting material must be found to protect children from boredom, anxiety and failure. Children are never passive listeners. In my own school children were encouraged to talk. The "news" session in our daily assembly from 9 a.m. to 9:30 a.m. was led by the children. Sometimes they would address the whole school; sometimes they would tell a "make-up" story. They were not inhibited in any way. The other children listened because they knew that when it came to their turn to talk they would want others to listen. The day in each classroom would begin with news—talking news and as they progressed, written news. Children shared their personal experiences with their class. They could talk freely to their teacher, knowing that she would listen. As head teacher, my door was always open as children arrived at school. I had a listening ear, and was, I am sure, often told family secrets. I remembered that as a small child I was too afraid to say very little except "yes" or "no."

Writing was part of this news. Children began every day with "news" recording. The teacher of the five-year-olds would get children to tell their news and then would write the most interesting item on a large newsheet. The children could then read the news and the words were written on a large wall dictionary, so that the children had a reference if the words were needed again. As they learned they would have their own "news" book in which to write and their own spelling books. Rosina Spitzer from the Montebello Intermediate School District visited my school and wrote an excellent article called "Why Johnnie Can Read." I quote from that document: "Children record their own thoughts and experiences daily. A 'speller' was another little blank book in which words were entered by the teacher, peers or themselves as they needed them for their own writing. I counted the words in six-year-old

Sharon's speller and found she had 350 words. Every day children wrote in their own books. The teacher's only request was that they began each day with a sentence telling about the weather. This ensured a way for them to get started and they had the option of writing more. This book brought the process into full action by thinking, writing, reading, and talking. They individually read their book to the teacher. This language experience approach meant that the children could write and read and they obviously enjoyed it. As they wrote, language flowed, ideas were exchanged and a vocabulary collected that would last a lifetime. The children had used every area of the curriculum—math, English, drama, poetry, science, arts and crafts. For some there was mystery, for some a miracle, but for all there was enjoyment in doing, talking, listening, reading, and writing. Every child is aware of the world in which he lives. He is filled with wonder—each day is a new adventure. There must be answers to satisfy his curiosity. Circumstances are contrived in which the child is encouraged and helped to 'find out' for itself."

I would say that writing comes easily to a child. In fact, I do not know which comes first, writing or reading. A child will pick up a stick on a sandy beach, write with it and tell you "what it says." Their early scribbles will say "something" and I have had letters from three-year-old nieces and nephews—a little like hieroglyphics with the message written on the back by Mum. Writing is part and parcel of learning to read. It is quite a different skill from reading and talking. When the child talks, usually there is a listener, someone who by their facial expression or interjections will stimulate the language. In writing there is a different situation. Most of the writing we get from children, in these early years is recorded speech. In written speech Vygotsky stated, "We create the situation and represent it to ourselves." Thus, when children write their "news" for us, this is exactly what they do. When children write, they are writing for themselves. It is true, it is expected that you will read it, but it is not the same as spoken language. The sequence of happenings, the subject matter, has to come from them. Another does not prompt it as the listener prompts in spoken language. The question might arise, why read at all, and for the child if there is no reader this must be even more true. I have found that the most important stimulus in getting a child to write is that I shall read it, comment and encourage. I attribute any success I may have with children's creative written work to the daily "news" writing. Written news, like spoken news, is a shared experience, and however busy the day, time should be spared to share it with the child. Newspapers would not be published if there were no readers, and the quality of the language and subject matter would soon deteriorate if nobody commented. I feel that we must read children's written work if we are to encourage them.

In my school we had a parents' assembly every Friday afternoon. After the assembly they would go to look at the things in the classroom that their children had done that week. I could guarantee that the first thing they would look at would be the news book. I quote from Brian's news. He was almost six years old.

"Today is Monday, September 25th. The wind is in the Northwest. The temperature is 60°. The weather is cold and sunny. My Dad died in the night and my Mummy went to church and David played with me and David's Mummy brought me to school and I told Mrs. Thompson all about my Dad, and I felt better."

His Mother told me years later that all the talking and writing we did together helped her small son through that very difficult time. The child says

> "What I can think about, I can talk about. What I can say, I can write—or someone else can write it for me.
>
> What I can write, I can read. I can read what I can write, and what other people write for me to read." This surely sums up the "harmonizing."

Getting children to write depends too on the actual skill. "I can't write anymore, my fingers ache." This can be a genuine excuse. My three and four year olds in the Nursery class are given lots of manipulative things to do with their hands—to build up finger muscles. Looking at the writing done by six and seven year olds, I found it was the children who had mastered the physical skill who spent most time in the Author's Corner. They wrote many books for their class library. Therefore, as early as possible we must help this physical skill by giving them plenty of interesting practice. "Interesting" rears its head. I can remember, how, as a child, "composition" was on the timetable. Our pencils would be sharpened, and their vicious looking points would be looking up at us. The virgin sheet of paper would be there, mocking, waiting for our mistakes and the teacher's red pen. She would write the title on the board. I dreaded those titles. I had so many imaginative stories in my head, just bursting to get out. She warned us about the perils that would befall us if the writing was not copperplate or there were too many spelling mistakes. With the fear of the teacher (only a little less than the fear of God) we would grasp the pencil and begin. There was nothing to stimulate our imaginations. No wonder our finger nails were bitten and our pencils chewed. We have, I hope, led children to write in a much happier way.

I quote a favorite poem. I once heard the poet, Leslie Norris, read it when I was a young teacher.

"The Thin Prison"

Hold the pen close to your ear,
Listen! Can you hear them?
Words, burning as a flame,
Words glittering like a tear.

Locked, all locked in the slim pen.
They are crying for freedom,
And you can release them,
Set them running from prison

Himalayas, balloons, Captain Cook
Kites, red bricks, London Town,
Sequins, cricket bats, large brown
Boots, lions and lemonade. Look!
I've just let them out!
Pick up your pen and start,

Think of the things you know - then
Let the words dance from your pen

I quoted this to my children year after year, when I wanted them to write for me. I would give them time to think. Often they would put their pencils to their ears. "You don't have to write it now," I would say. "Think about it when you go to bed tonight, and when you have a good story, go into the Author's Corner and write it. You can make it into a book, illustrate it, and the rest of the class can read it." I would hover around the author praising, encouraging and give help when it was needed. In the early years when I came to Conference I would bring dozens of these books to share with teachers. Some, I feel sure, could hardly believe that such young children had written them.

Children can only write if there is something to write about. A word of warning here. We must be aware of the practice of taking children on visits for the sole purpose of getting them to write about it. "Will we have to write about it when we get back Miss?" "Yes." "Then I don't want to go." I may have been guilty of doing these years ago but I learned not to do this. I can remember how sad I was when I first went to San Diego Zoo many years ago and saw children who should have been enjoying the visit, encumbered with paper and pencil, and worried because they had to answer all the questions. Imagine it! "How many legs has an elephant?" The child was so busy counting the legs, it didn't see the shape of the animal, the texture of the its skin, or the look in the elephant's eye.

Writing isn't just recording. There are so many ways to interest and stimulate the child. The boy who can pretend to be a newspaper reporter and can go into the Newspaper Office in the corner of the classroom has advantage over the child who is told to sit and get on with it. My class newspaper the *Express & Sun* covered such a wide field of interests and was an excellent way to interest not only the class but other classes and parents. The class magazine did the same. These literary efforts were very worthwhile. If there was an end product the children were always keen. Drama encouraged them to write scripts and act. I wish I had space to record some of the "plays" that were written and acted out by my children. The older children in the school wrote ten sentence stories for the younger children. They would put a sentence on a page and illustrate it on the next. These were often used as "reading books" by my five-year-olds. Writing to relatives and other children gave them an incentive to write especially when I would provide stamps so that they could mail them. I can hear the conscientious teacher asking about "corrections." I did want good writing and good spelling. Writing came from practicing the skill and spelling was learned by using words in context. I would make sure they used their own "speller" wordbook which became their property as they moved up through the classes. I had respect for the child's creative writing as I would have for any picture that it painted. I would discuss the grammar and spelling with the child and allow them to erase and correct their own work. In this way the correction had meaning because it was given in a one-to-one situation and was more easily memorized. In all the child's writing then has been "thinking" put down on paper, talking and reading to anyone who will listen. Harmonizing many voices.

Reading to many means those awful primers and reading schemes. Often the publishers are the only ones who benefit. No wonder children can't wait to escape from those books. As a young teacher I was often asked to lecture by HM Inspectors on how I managed to get my children to read so well. I would talk about the variety of books I used to suit the individual child, the classroom environment, the fun of reading games and pre-reading activities, the floor books, wall stories, books written by the child to read to Mum and Dad and just when I thought I had exhausted all the ideas a voice from the back of the room would say, "What about the bottom group?"

In a flash I would see that other classroom, where children were grouped and non-readers singled out for special attention. You would be reminded that the child would be called out to read "a page a day"— barking at print. Children would read round the class. One would read whilst the rest of the class listened, keeping a finger on each word as it was read. I would have to answer that question with a question.

"What about your bottom group? How do you cope?" I ask.
"Well," comes the reply, "I hear them read every day."
"Does that help?" I ask.
"Not much, but it eases my conscience," comes the reply.

I can picture the situation. That bottom group still reading, "Come, come, come. Come and look."

I think of the child who daily faces failure, who waits with a sinking heart for the moment when the teacher calls him out to read. The teacher faced with those same books day after day, year after year, must pass on her boredom to the child. She will "fit in" these failures at any time convenient to her, playtime as she sips her tea; or when the others are having PE or games. Poor old "bottom grouper" might like some PE or games. My next question:

"What do you do when he comes to the end of the book, and you are not satisfied that he has read the book?"

"I make him start at the beginning again," she replies.

You can't make him read, but she as his teacher has the authority to make him read what she chooses for him, so he starts at the beginning again.

My next question:

"Have you got a woodwork bench?" "Yes" comes the reply, "but it is only used by the good readers who have time to spare."

Having missed out on playtime, PE and games, he now misses out on woodwork, perhaps a very important activity in the life of the slow reader.

"Well," I say, "I have often found that I get a slow reader to read a book he has written for himself, when he has rejected all other books. He will need your help of course, and your time, which I am sure you give freely every day. When you hear him stumble over those words in his primer—get him excited about wood and nails. Get him to draw a simple object like an aeroplane, and then let him make it. As he works, you can daily record what is happening. He will have written a book, albeit with a lot of help from you."

One such book I made with Philip.

Page 1	My name is Philip
Page 2	This is an aeroplane. I am going to make it
Page 3	I have some wood
Page 4	I have some nails
Page 5	I have a hammer and saw
Page 6	I cut some wood for the aeroplane
Page 7	I saw some wood for the wings
Page 8	I saw a piece of wood for the tail
Page 9	I nail them together
Page 10	I sandpaper my aeroplane
Page 11	I paint my aeroplane red and blue
Page 12	I can take my book home to show my Mum and Dad

He made the book covers and together we wrote:

> How to make an aeroplane
> Written by Philip
> Published by Mrs Thompson

Philip knew all about his book. He wanted to show it and read it to everybody. Nothing succeeds like success and how much more interesting for him to read about what he had done. He had the moment of great joy when he said, "I can read this. It is easy. Listen to me. What shall I make next?"

I don't know whether my questioner let her "bottom groupers" use the woodwork bench. You can lead a horse to water but you cannot make it drink!

If when we used the public library we were given any old book to read, how many of us would go again? David in my class regularly used a Sporting Newspaper as his reading book. Every Monday he followed his one and only interest, football. All week he read that paper. He struggled with team names until he mastered them. Not only was he keen to read but his geography and general knowledge was built into the process. One day with added confidence he discovered that those books in the book corner were not as dull as he thought they were when he was a non-reader. He began to take books home to share with his Mum and Dad.

Reading matter for children should be linked from the beginning to their own spoken language. The child's neighborhood dialect may well be the only resource he brings to learning to read and write. We must separate the idea of teaching reading from how reading is learned. We must forget sometimes how to teach and remember how we learned. The teaching of rules, graphemes, morphemes, correspondences and all the various skills is, if not totally ineffective, certainly excessively inefficient. Reading is often a silent act. Watching children read, we only see the tip of the iceberg. We see their eyes move. We must give children more time to read rather than testing them to see if they have read. Reading is individual in nature. It is a personal experience and writing and reading emerge concurrently. We must remember that children learn naturally and know a lot about literacy before they come to school. All children can learn and they learn best when learning is meaningful, interesting and functional. They certainly learn best when many voices are harmonized. Literacy develops before children start formal instruction. It develops in real life settings for real activities in order to get things done. Children learn to write by writing and to read by reading. Graham Greene in *Lost Childhood* writes, "Perhaps it is only in childhood that books have a deep influence on our lives. In childhood, all books and books of divination telling us about the future, and like the fortune-teller, who sees a long journey ahead in the cards, or death by drowning, they influence the future. I suppose that is why books excited us so much. What do we ever get nowadays to equal the excitement and revelation of those first fourteen years?"

Roald Dahl, who has excited so many children with his books, stated, "The prime function of the children's book writer is to write a book that is so absorbing, exciting, fast, funny and beautiful that the child will fall in love with it. And that first love affair between the young child and the young book will hopefully lead to other loves for other books and when that happens the battle is probably won. The child will have found a crock of gold. He will also have gained something that will help to carry him most miraculously through the tangles of his later years."

There have never been so many wonderful books for children to read. Orville Prescott wrote and as teachers we must note the truth of it, "Few children learn to love books by themselves. Someone has to lure them into the wonderful world of the written word. Someone has to show them the way."

We can excite children by reading and telling them stories. A story has real power.

> Taste a story
> Touch it,
> Try it.
> Tell a story
> Sell it,
> Buy it.
> Laugh a story,
> Feel it,
> Cry it.
> Talk with it
> Walk with it
> And, when you know your story well
> Go, fly with it!

There must be something between the covers of the book to make children want to read those stories in the book corner. Not only stories but also all the other things a child wants to know. I remember Jeremy who advised me to get more books on space as he had read them all!

As a young teacher I had 65 children in my class and a head teacher who said I had to hear every child read every day. I would put them in circles, start them off on page 21 and then go round as they read. I could honestly say I had heard every child read. Reading is an activity that goes on throughout the whole day in a good classroom. With an integrated day, children are working individually at their own activities and can choose which to tackle first. They were conditioned and expected to accomplish every activity. Studying my children and remembering I really could see the "harmonizing of many voices."

I seem to have rambled on, as I usually do about listening, talking, writing and reading. I could write books at length about each of them but there would be an overlap, as they could not be discussed separately. They are all part of the thing we call "literacy." We encourage our children, we know they learn to talk by hearing other people talk, they learn to write by reading what they have written, they absorb the vocabulary and the sentence structures, and the forms of poetry; stories, essays, recipes and all the other many types of writing by seeing them on the page. Shakespeare owed much to Roman authors, TS Elliot to the Elizabethans, Ted Hughes, our poet laureate, to DH Lawrence, Beatrix Potter revealed her sources as have many others. Exposing our children to literacy and inspiring them to "harmonize" we can be assured that they will become literate human beings. As a teacher that is my hope. It's a wonderful thing, education!

READING AND WRITING ALL DAY LONG IN THE K-1 CLASSROOM

Rozanne Lanczak Williams

A Word About How Children Acquire Literacy

Everything I've learned about how children learn to read and write comes from my experiences as a classroom teacher, as writer and editor for educational materials, as a parent of three children, and from my close and continuing collaboration with K-1 teachers. One of my core beliefs regarding early literacy acquisition is based on the premise that young children must be given many and varied opportunities to read and write throughout the school day. To try to accomplish this, many teachers find themselves frustrated when they "try to do it all," that is, get their children reading and writing as well as fitting in all the other goodies including science, math, social studies, music, art, P.E., character education.... Doesn't the list seem to go on and on? In addressing many teachers' concerns, I would like to share some ways to create a powerful, primary program by integrating reading and writing in the content areas.

Integrating Reading and Writing in the Content Areas— A Balanced Approach

Reading Aloud Time

Gather fiction and nonfiction literature books for daily read-alouds related to your focus unit in the content area. For example, if you are planning a science unit on weather, appropriate read-aloud books might include *Weather Words and What They Mean* by Gail Gibbons, or *Storms* by Seymour Simon. Read-aloud books for a social studies unit on homes and shelters could include: *Houses and Homes* by Ann Morris (Mulberry) and *Homes Around the World* by Bobbie Kalman (Crabtree). Over the past several years, an incredible number of quality literature books have been published with science, social studies, and math themes. Make friends with your school or public librarian and your local bookseller to find the newest and best books available that relate to your units of study. Share resources with your teaching partners to expand your choices.

During read-aloud time, children gain information and knowledge that they can access when working on their own, in their writing, or when working on projects. Children in any classroom (graded or multi-age) are at different developmental levels in thinking, reading, and writing skills. By reading aloud, you are reaching *all* children and are allowing them to participate in the discussion on their own level. Read-aloud time is also a good time to add to your charts titled, "What do we know?" "What do we want to know?" and "What did we learn?" Always recycle read-aloud books by featuring them in class centers related to your content area focus or the class library corner. The books can be a source of reading material for fluent readers as well as resources for hands-on projects. For example, children can refer to the books about homes mentioned above to make models of houses people live in around the world.

Shared Reading

Shared reading provides the opportunity to teach reading strategies. By choosing shared reading material that relates to your content area focus, an extra level of learning is added. Invite children to join in as you read poems, Big Books, pocket charts, and when you sing together. Write text from your shared reading material on sentence strips for a class read-along using the pocket chart. Write text from Big Books that can be sung on charts for a class sing-along. Children use their knowledge gained from read-alouds, along with the patterned language found in shared reading material, to extend both learning in the content areas and reading skill development.

Some examples of books appropriate for shared reading during a weather unit are: *Rain* by Robert Kalan (Greenwillow); *It Looked Like Spilt Milk* by Charles G. Shaw (HarperCollins) or *What's the Weather Like Today?* by Rozanne Lanczak Williams (Creative Teaching Press).

Refer to the text in shared reading materials relating to your focus units and create class-made big books, individual student books or wall stories. By creating innovations to the original text, students can practice as well as extend their reading skills. These materials can also serve as resource books to extend children's knowledge and vocabulary in the content areas. For example, after singing "Over in the Meadow" as a shared reading activity, create a science big book featuring other habitats. Here's an example of one verse:

Over in the ocean in the deep blue sea
Lived a pod of whales. Can you count three?
"Swim deep, whales!" "We swim!" said the three.
So they swam all day in the deep blue sea."

Guided Reading

Finding the right books to match the reading level of children assigned to guided-reading groups is a challenge. Deviating from your focus study in the content area is standard practice in guided reading. However, by scouring your collections of guided reading books, and enlisting the help of your curriculum specialist, learning specialist, or mentor teacher, you will be able to find some material suitable for guided reading that relates to your focus theme. Some titles for guided reading during a weather unit might include: *The Storm* by Jillian Cutting (The Wright Group); *What's the Weather?* by Rozanne Lanczak Williams (Creative Teaching Press) or the *The Wind Blew* by Pat Hutchins (Greenwillow).

Keep 'Em Reading . . .
Keep 'Em Writing . . .
Keep 'Em Learning . . .

Because rereading is so important, place books from shared and guided reading, along with books the children have made, in centers and the class library. Rereading gives readers a chance to experience the text in different ways as well and helps them become more fluent readers. Revisit the books once again by tapping into their content when doing project work (class informational big books, models, reports, experiments, etc.).

Books children make in the classroom provide an especially treasured and meaningful source of additional reading material. Integrate reading and writing in the content areas by making books containing math, science, and social studies concepts. Sources of text for student-made books include:

- Innovations of shared reading material (Big Books, pocket charts, wall stories, etc.)
- Reproducible emergent readers
- Traditional poems, songs, rhymes & chants
- Children's published work
- Stories written during shared reading time
- Language experience stories

Have lots of writing and art supplies available to students. Shared reading books and texts will inspire beginner writers to create their own versions of favorite stories. During an integrated science unit, one student, on her own, took dark blue construction paper and white paint and wrote her own version of *It Looked Like Spilt Milk* (Harper). Another child followed the patterned language in *The Four Seasons* (Creative Teaching Press) to create a wonderful book with the following text:

> *It's Spring. I see baseballs and bats!*
> *It's Summer. I see swimming pools.*
> *It's Fall. I see soccer balls.*
> *It's Winter. I see sleds and boots.*

At the start of the school year, invite children to make home book boxes. After children have read their hand-made books several times, they can take them home to keep in their special boxes. What a great way to supply reading material in the home and to encourage home reading! All the little books made during the year and stored in the book box provide a wonderful collection for summer reading.

Encourage writing throughout the day by providing children with math and science journals or clipboards on which to write when taking walks outdoors or when going on field trips. Also supply blank books and response sheets to accompany class projects.

In closing . . . .

I hope that by sharing ways to integrate literacy learning in the content areas, you will be able to implement your own program customized to your students' needs. Skills and knowledge will naturally grow when children are given many opportunities to read and write all through the day.

Resources for Teacher

Ball, L., and Brucker, L. (1998). *Look! Look! I Wrote a Book!* Glenview, IL: Good Year Books.

Jordano, K. (1997). *Home and Back with Books*. Cypress, CA: Creative Teaching Press.

Williams, R. L. (1998). *Make Your Own Emergent Readers*, *8-Book Series*. Torrance, CA: Frank Schaffer Publications.

_____. (1998). *Phonics Pocket Books and Kits for Emergent Readers*. Santa Rosa, CA: Sue Lewis Publications.

WHAT DO YOU MEAN I SHOULD TEACH READING TO SECONDARY STUDENTS?

Claire V. Sibold

Mr. Peralto accompanies Jason, a sophomore at Roosevelt High School, through a typical day at school. At the end of Jason's first period Biology class, the teacher calls on Jason to read aloud. Reluctantly, Jason begins reads a page of the text on the structure of molds; then the bell rings. He rushes to his second American History class. As he is listening to the teacher, he becomes confused about the difference between the branches of government. The teacher continues to lecture, answering only of few questions posed by those who have raised their hands. Jason thinks to himself, "I hate history, it's so boring," and he is relieved when class ends. He looks forward to his next class, Computer Applications, where he excels. The teacher gives an assignment for students to complete and, without any hesitation, Jason begins working.

Jason is typical of high school students who must transition quickly from one content area to the next. Students encounter several challenges—the demands of reading aloud, disinterest in the course content, a mismatch between his learning style and the teaching method, incomprehensibility due to a lack of prior experience, and the concept load. These are just a few reasons why students struggle in content subjects. Teachers can help their students become content literate in the subjects they teach.

Content literacy is a student's ability to use reading and writing to learn subject matter in a given discipline. To be literate in content area classrooms, students must learn how to use reading and writing to explore and construct meaning. All too often textbooks are viewed as sacred canons or authoritative sources of knowledge from which students learn new information. Teachers may assume that high school students are proficient readers or view their own role as disseminators of information. Therefore, content teachers may not provide sufficient help to readers who cannot understand the material.

However, teachers can play a critical role in helping students learn with text. It doesn't require teachers to become reading teachers, but it does require a change in his/her thinking. It does not diminish the teacher's role as a content specialist. In fact, the content teacher's expertise enables her/him make choices about the types of strategies s/he wishes to use to enhance students' ability to learn the material.

Some strategies assist students at the pre-reading stage and allow them to utilize their existing schemata and develop independent strategies to maximize learning from the text. "Preparation is the basis for comprehension. If [students are] not prepared or expectant, [their] understanding will suffer" (Richardson & Morgan, 1990, p. 115). Teachers can prepare students for reading by finding out what they know and/or building background.

Other strategies are designed to guide students as they read a text selection, poem, or fictional or non-fictional selection. Study guides, the "W" in the K-W-L strategy, and dialogue journals are just a few of these. Still others help students construct meaning after they have read. Semantic mapping, summaries, and the "L" in the K-W-L strategy, and class discussions help students to reflect upon what they have learned and construct meaning.

The following four strategies—Anticipation Guide, Q-A-R Strategy, EVOKER, and the Sell Technique—can enhance students' comprehension of content subject matter. It is important to note that these strategies can be adapted for use with reading materials, lectures, videotapes, or demonstrations.

Anticipation Guide

The Anticipation Guide allows students to explore their preconceived ideas and knowledge before they read content material, listen to a lecture, or watch a video. "The Anticipation Guide attempts to enhance students' comprehension by having them react to a series of statements about a topic before they begin to read..." (Tierney, Readence, & Dishner, 1990, p. 45). The strategy fosters discussion after the students have interacted with information. This guide can be adapted to different subject areas and media. The teacher can construct statements to tap students' preconceived ideas or uncover their prior knowledge and help them anticipate what they will encounter.

To implement the strategy, the teacher instructs the students to read each statement and determines if s/he agrees or disagrees with the statement. The students then check the blank under Agree or Disagree. At this point, the teacher may discuss the statements or the student may go ahead and read the text selection. After reading the selection, the students read the statements again. To foster discussion, the teacher may ask, "Did any of your ideas change?" "With which statements do you now Agree or Disagree?" True or False may be used in place of Agree or Disagree.

Table I is an example of how secondary students can adapt this type of guide to assist them in a understanding a selection from a science textbook for eighth grade students. The purpose of this Anticipation Guide is to determine what the students already know about the structure of mold. After reading the selection, students return to the five statements and determine with which ones s/he now agrees.

Table I
Anticipation Guide: *The Structure of Mold*

Agree   Disagree

____   ____   1. Mold causes food to spoil, such as apples, granola bars, cheeses, and oranges.

____   ____   2. When a spore case bursts, it shoots out spores which then fall onto food and grow into a fully ripened mold.

____   ____   3. Some molds are useful in making special cheeses.

____   ____   4. Substances made from molds can kill germs and stop infection.

____   ____   5. Louis Pasteur discovered that some bacteria growing on seaweed seemed to dissolve (Oxenhorn, 1975, pp. 36-40).

K-W-L Strategy

The K-W-L Strategy incorporates all three stages of reading—pre-reading, reading, and post-reading. The teacher determines what the students already "know" and builds upon this knowledge prior to assigning the reading selection, watching a video, or listening to a lecture. S/He asks, "What do you know about _____?" It is helpful to use a chart and list what the students know in the first column. Then, the entire class considers what they want to find out as they read, watch, or listen. They formulate questions that the teacher writes in the column under "Want to Find Out." These questions can be categorized and used as a guide as students read, view, or listen. "When students look for something as they study, they usually find it. When they look for nothing, they usually find it too!" (Herber & Herber, 1993, p. 123). After the students read, for example, the class can recall what they've learned and the teacher can record their ideas in the last column to indicated what they have "Learned."

For example, middle school students are going to read a short selection and see a video on *The Gray Wolf.* The teacher can find out what his/her students already know about wolves, find out what they want to find out, and later discuss what they learned. In their cooperative learning groups, the students will research one of the four categories—socialization, mating habits, communication, and physical characteristics. This information will be shared with the entire class. Table II shows some of the ideas generated by middle school students.

Question-Answer Relationship Strategy

The Question-Answer Relationships (QARS) "[enhances] students' ability to answer comprehension questions by giving them a systematic means for analyzing task demands of different questions probes" (Tierney, Readence, Dishner, 1990, p. 61). This strategy is useful with both fiction and non-fiction. There are four types of questions: Right There, Think and Search, Author and Me, and On My Own. However, teachers may choose to use all or only a few of these four types of questions.

Table II

An Example of How Students Use the KWL Strategy.

KNOW	WANT TO FIND OUT	LEARNED
They are predators. They hunt small animals. Wolves howl at the moon. They live in dense forests. They kill farm animals.	What are their mating habits? How long do they live? How many travel in a pack? Are wolves endangered? How do they communicate?	They make long, mournful sounds. They hunt in packs. There are 8-10 wolves in a pack. The pack is a social unit. The leader of the wolf pack is called the alpha.
Categories: Socialization Mating habits Communication Physical characteristics		

"Right There" questions require the reader to recall information. However, if a student does not know the answer, s/he can locate an answer by going to the text and find the answer. Many of these questions begin with words such as what, who, when. "Author and Me" questions include both what the student already knows and the author's ideas. The student "Think and Search" questions move students to a higher level of thinking and require students to make inferences, pull information together from different parts of the selection, translate information, or analyze the contents. To respond to questions "On My Own," students move outside the text. The answer does not appear in the reading selection. The student draws from his/her own experiences and prior knowledge.

To implement this strategy, the teacher provides direct instruction and gives examples of questions for each of four levels. It is important to show the response demands of each question type and walk the

students through the procedure. Here are some sample questions related
to this article. First read the question, then consider what the response
demands are for the question. Finally, carefully phrase your answer.

Right There: What are the three parts of the K-W-L strategy?

Between the Lines: Which of these strategies can be used at the
pre-reading stage?

Beyond the Lines: What other strategies have you used that
enhanced student learning in your content area classroom?

Writer and Me: Which of the strategies presented would be most
applicable to the subjects you teach? Why?

Which of these questions was easiest to answer? Why? Which was
the most difficult? Why? These questions help students provide the
teacher with feedback as s/he determines how the student is processing
the question and answer.

EVOKER Study Method

The EVOKER study method is a meaning-making strategy that is
used primarily with poetry and prose selections to help students explore
the selection in depth but in an organized fashion. The EVOKER is a 6-
step study method and a guide that, once modeled, can be used
independently while students read an unfamiliar selection. EVOKER
stands for Explore, Vocabulary, Oral Reading, Key Ideas, Evaluate, and
Recapitulate. Steps 2 through 5 can be repeated in class as a post-reading
strategy.

The following steps will help the English teacher and his/her
students implement this strategy:

1. Explore - The students will read the selection quietly on their own.

2. Vocabulary - The students then note the words they do not
   understand. The teacher can also add the words she feels are key to
   the passage.

3. Oral Reading - The students read the selection aloud in groups, pairs, or as an entire class.

4. Key Ideas - The teacher and students identify the selection's main idea or theme. It may be helpful to outline the key points or arrange them into a graphic organizer.

5. Evaluate - The class can further evaluate the key words and phrases identified in step 2 to help develop the poet's or author's main ideas discussed in step 4.

6. Recapitulate - The class reads the selection for a third time, now with a better understanding of the selection (Readence, Bean, & Baldwin, p. 265).

Sell Technique

The purpose of the Sell Technique is to help students read and understand content information thoroughly and to assist their peers by "selling" what they have learned to others (Anderson, 1997). This technique helps students process information. To implement this strategy, use the following steps:

1. The teacher assigns a selection for students to read in depth, e.g., a passage, article, or chapter.

2. As each student reads the selection, the student tries to think about what is important about the selection.

3. After reading, the student writes three questions to ask her/his peers.

4. The class is divided into groups of three; and then each person in the group alternates asking questions while the others think and respond to each question. If the other students do not have a clear understanding of the information, the student who posed the question explains the information more completely.

The teacher can roam between groups and record the names of the students responding to the question. There are two ways to evaluate the students throughout this process. First, the teacher can evaluate group members' responses to the questions posed and also provide points for answering questions and writing their own questions. Secondly, the teacher can evaluate the quality of the questions and written answers provided by each student. In other words, the teacher should encourage students to write critical level thinking questions and write a complete answer.

The advantage of the Sell Technique is that the student chooses materials that the student feels are important. Keys to the success of this technique are providing sample questions for students at a variety of comprehension levels, careful record-keeping, and varying the use of the strategy so students do not tire of the technique.

The Sell Technique allows preservice teachers in a secondary reading methods course at Biola University to process what they have learned from a chapter and also practice writing questions at different levels of Bloom's taxonomy. For example, this technique has been particularly successful with the preservice teachers. Here are some sample questions developed from the material in Chapter 8 (Vacca & Vacca, 1996, pp. 248-278).

1. Comprehension: Describe the basic elements of story structure.

2. Application: Use one of the text frames with graphic representations formats in Chapter 8 to show how you would introduce a topic in a unit you teach.

3. Analysis: Examine a page in the social science textbook enclosed. Identify the predominant text pattern.

The professor divides the class into groups of three and places slips of paper with the three different levels written on them in an envelope in front of each group. The students withdraw a slip of paper to determine which of their three questions they will share. Beginning with the comprehension level, each student poses his/her question to the group. The other two students respond to the question. If the students do not answer the question clearly, then the student who posed the question "sells" the information to the others.

The Sell Technique may be graded in three ways: (1) the quality of the questions and complete responses; (2) the teaching/explanation of the information, or correct; and/or (3) thoughtful responses to the questions posed by others. Students who are selling the information should be instructed to know the answer and not read the answer. The professor observes and records who is responding to the questions in each group.

There are a variety of strategies for introducing selections, assisting students as they read, and constructing meaning. Additional strategies to consider are Focus Questions, DRTA (directed reading-thinking activity), ReQuest Procedure, the Herringbone Technique, a CD Map, graphic organizers, Guided Writing Procedure, and Think-Sheets for comparing and contrasting ideas (Tierney, Readence, Dishner, 1990; Vacca & Vacca, 1996). Students ... "who are less than fluent in English pose a considerable challenge for teachers. Guiding these students toward successful reading experiences is a task that more and more teachers face" (Chen & Graves, 1998, p. 570). By building anticipation, setting purposes for reading, and incorporating comprehension strategies into instruction, secondary students with differing abilities will be more successful in their content classes.

References

Anderson, C. (1997, August). The Role of the Professor in Retention. Paper presented at the Faculty Workshop at Biola University, La Mirada, CA.

Chen, H. S., and Graves, M. (1998). "Previewing Challenging Reading Selections for ESL Students." *Journal of Adolescent and Adult Literacy*, 41 (7), pp. 570-571.

Herber, H. L, and Herber, J. N. (1993). *Teaching in Content Areas With Reading, Writing, and Reasoning.* Needham Heights, MA: Allyn and Bacon.

Irwin, J. W. (1991). *Teaching Reading Comprehension Processes* (2nd ed.). Englewood Cliffs, NJ: Prentice-Hall, pp. 45-49.

McKenna, M. C., and Robinson, R. D. (1993). *Teaching Through Text.* NY: Longman.

Oxenhorn, J. M. (1975). *Pathways to Science.* NY: Globe.

Readence, J. E., Bean, T. W., and Baldwin, R.S . (1992). *Content Area Reading: An Integrated Approach* (4th ed.). Dubuque, IA: Kendall/Hunt.

Richardson, J. S., and Morgan, R. F. (1990). *Reading to Learn in the Content Areas*. Belmont, CA: Wadsworth.

Tierney, R. J., Readence, J. E., and Dishner, E. K. (1990). *Reading Strategies And Practices: A Compendium*. Needham Heights, MA: Allyn and Bacon.

Vacca, R. T., and Vacca, L. (1996). *Content Area Reading* (5th Ed). NY: Harper Collins.

DEVELOPING MAINSTREAM DISCOURSE SKILLS IN SECOND LANGUAGE STUDENTS: WHAT A DIFFERENCE A CRITICAL CONSCIOUSNESS MAKES

Evangelina Bustamante Jones

To begin with, this is not what I mean when I use the term *mainstream discourse skills*:

Welcome to ESL 101, English Surely Latinized,
inglés con chile y cilantro, English as American
as Benito Juárez. Welcome, muchachos from
      Xochicalco,
learn the language of dólares* and dolores**, of kings
and queens, of Donald Duck and Batman. Holy Toluca!
In four months you'll be speaking like George
      Washington,
in four weeks you can ask, More coffee? In two months
you can say, May I take your order? In one year you
can ask for a raise, cool as the Tuxpan River.
      *dollars   **pains
(from "English con Salsa," by Gina Valdés, 1994, p. 3)

I am not referring to *functional literacy*, which serves to provide a large supply of low-skilled workers in order to ease the lives of more privileged folk. I am not proposing the development of mainstream discourse skills as a way of alienating students from their primary languages, communities, cultures, or values in order to embrace assimilation into the larger society. Instead, I see mainstream discourse skills as instrumental in the re-creation of society so that it can become a true cultural democracy (Darder, 1991). This perspective is supported by my research on exemplary teachers of color and their literacy practices.

In this paper, I intend to explain how discourse skills can be taught through critically conscious literacy practices. I will also describe a research-based format (Chamot & O'Malley, 1994) that can be used as a guide for assessing and planning the development of content literacy, and illustrate how its components align with some of the foundational principles of literacy instruction that the teachers in my research study used in their teaching.

Mainstream Discourse Skills and Literate Discourse

The teaching and learning of mainstream discourse skills in classrooms full of second language learners and other non-mainstream students have too often been nothing more than decontextualized bits of language to be mastered through skills-based instruction informed by standardized test items. Non-mainstream students are placed in tracked, remedial-based management systems that are supposed to produce functional literates to fit into ever-expanding technological workplaces (Macedo, 1991; Shannon, 1990). Such literacy instruction is tied to mechanical, not critical literacy (Macedo, 1991). However, according to Gee (1991), literacy is much more than components of language; literacy is embedded within a larger political entity, which he calls a discourse. One's beliefs and values shape the way one writes, talks, and reads. Primary discourses are learned in the homes and communities, but secondary discourses (synonymous with literate discourses) are associated with groups or institutions encountered later, most usually through formal schooling (Gee, 1991). The discourses of lawyers, academics, political leaders, or computer technologists are examples. Secondary discourses are associated with different levels of status, as well as social and/or economic power.

It is also the case that a person's status level who is "born into a particular discourse tends to be maintained because primary discourses are related to secondary discourses of similar status in our society (for example, the middle-class home discourse to school discourse, or the working class African-American home discourse to the black church discourse)" (Delpit, 1995, p. 153). People without the more powerful discourses are excluded when they do not "pass" tests of fluency in the dominant discourses; in these tests, what counts are surface features of language, not content (Gee, cited in Delpit, 1995). The power wielded in this society by privileged groups who "own" the high status, literate discourses can be seen in the way that language is used to define, categorize, exclude--or include--people (Gee, 1991).

How will students who are born into a "particular" discourse acquire one that will allow them to enter into the powerful, high-status discourses? Must they use the survival strategy called "racelessness" (Fordham, 1988), thereby setting themselves apart from their own communities to do so, or can they retain their cultural and ethnic identities, while keeping and enjoying the warmth of their primary discourses?

How Exemplary Teachers of Color View Literacy Instruction

It is important to learn from individuals who have been able to acquire the powerful discourses of this society without losing their primary ones. To engage and negotiate in the community and mainstream cultures, and to deal with the contradictions and complex dissonance between them is to experience biculturalism (Darder, 1991). The insights of teachers of color who share similar lived experiences with their students and who are successful in promoting academic achievement can be instrumental in guiding the practice of teachers who do not have first-hand knowledge about their students' multiple realities. In the following passage, Lisa Delpit (1995), an African American educator, reveals that the school practices of critically conscious teachers of color are derived from what the parents and children in marginalized communities want:

> First, they know that members of society need access to dominant discourse to (legally) have access to economic power. Second, they know that such discourses can be and have been acquired in classrooms because they know individuals who have done so. And third, and most significant to the point I wish to make now, they know that individuals have the ability to transform dominant discourses for liberatory purposes—to engage in what Henry Louis Gates calls "changing the joke and slipping the yoke," that is, using European philosophical and critical standards to challenge the tenets of European belief systems (p.162)....[R]acism and oppression must be fought on as many fronts and in as many voices as we can muster (p. 163).

My research involving exemplary bicultural teachers resulted in a conceptual framework, "The Teacher of Color as Cultural Mediator," that both describes and elaborates upon Delpit's thesis (Jones, 1998). I examined research literature about exemplary teachers of color for recurrent themes, then conducted qualitative case studies of three fourth grade teachers who had been born and/or raised in the Mexican American community of Calexico, California where they were now teaching. My hope was that I would be able to study teachers who mirrored their students' sociocultural and socioeconomic characteristics, and to see how their bicultural identity and consciousness informed their teaching ideologies.

Through methods that included classroom observations, teacher interviews, and descriptive statistics of teacher/student interactions during literacy instruction using a classroom observation rubric, I identified the fundamental principles the three teachers held and how these were evident in their literacy instruction. The teachers' beliefs emanated from a fusion of two dimensions of their lived experiences. First, they possessed a bicultural or critical consciousness (Darder, 1991); they recognized the effects of power from the larger society and its impact on their primary language and culture. As children, they had experienced racism, low expectations, and hegemonic school practices that tried to marginalize them. Fortunately and ironically, it was their strong cultural values and pride in their language that helped them survive. Second, they possessed a deep knowledge of socioculturally-based cognition patterns, socially-appropriate learning contexts, and culturally valued knowledge (Hollins, 1996) of the Mexican culture in general and the community's norms and values in particular. Together, the interactions of these two dimensions resulted in a firm set of principles that drove their ideologies of teaching children who resembled them. These principles are: Bicultural Affirmation, Codes of Power, and Status Equalization.

Bicultural affirmation involves the interplay between the two cultures in the lives of the students. This interplay was illustrated particularly by the importance of role modeling and the utilization of students' cultural strengths in the classrooms. The three teachers operated as role models who could successfully and positively engage in the two community linguistic and cultural systems. The classrooms themselves reflected community cultural values, normative behaviors, and social expectations within the school's cultural capital, in effect producing an academic identity harmonious with the students' ethnic identities.

Codes of power is a term used by Delpit (1988) to mean the features of "linguistic forms, communicative strategies, and presentation of self; that is, ways of talking, ways of writing, ways of dressing, and ways of interacting" (p. 283). The teachers apportioned a great deal of time to teaching events, academic tasks, and academic products that raised the students' level of competency in mainstream discourse (in both languages), and enlarged the students' repertoire of cognitive strategies, skills, and power genres used in academic environments. Students understood the connection between attaining control of literacy, academic success, and the opportunities that would be available to them in the near future. Because of the biculturally affirming environment that supported their positive academic identities, students demonstrated a high degree of participation in, and acceptance of, the literacy tasks at hand.

Status equalization was evident through issues of language and control. The teachers articulated and demonstrated an ideology that used biliteracy and self-regulation as both the means and the ends in their classrooms. The valuing of biliteracy reflected an equitable relationship between the two languages of the students' world. The goal of self-regulation implied that the students were perceived as capable of being anything they wanted to be, i.e., successful scholars on their way to college. There was a strong future orientation in the classrooms, with self-regulation as an essential component.

While I recognize that my research study cannot be generalizable to situations in which the teachers and students do not belong to the same linguistic and cultural groups, the principles upon which the exemplary teachers in my study and in the research literature based their teaching can be used as a means to evaluate teaching and learning contexts elsewhere. In the following section, I will begin by describing an instructional format, the Cognitive Academic Language Learning Approach (CALLA) (Chamot & O'Malley, 1994), that I use in a content area reading methods course for middle school and high school pre-service teachers; then I will analyze its components through two of the principles found in my study, codes of power and status equalization. The principle of bicultural affirmation is a difficult one to apply in environments that do not feature the degree of community and district-wide adherence to the value of biculturalism as was found in the setting of Calexico.

The Development of Academic Language and Processes

Several resources exist that are useful for supporting the growth of academic language and processes, also known as cognitive academic language proficiency (CALP) (Cummins, 1979). Sheltered instruction, or Specially Designed Academic Instruction in English (SDAIE), offers a structure for delivering cognitively demanding content-based lessons to students whose English has progressed to the intermediate level of proficiency (Peregoy & Boyle, 1997).

It has been my experience, however, that although sheltered classes provide content through effectively contextualized means, such as visuals, graphic organizers, videos, hands-on activities, and paraphrasing of difficult-to-read texts, they do not also systematically provide students opportunities to engage thoughtfully and critically in the types of academic processes and products that are central to the specific content. Instructors are understandably focused on seeing that students comprehend the material. However, a student who successfully learns concepts in a life science SDAIE class might move on to a mainsteam science course, but not know how to organize, plan, or communicate her ideas and knowledge in the appropriate format. This in turn could prevent her from continuing in more advanced science courses, and consequently halt plans for college. In summary, these instructional approaches often result in transmission of knowledge, but they do not provide the tools to develop literate discourse at the level needed for higher academic achievement.

The Cognitive Academic Language Learning Approach (CALLA) (Chamot & O'Malley, 1994) does provide a comprehensive format that, if used as a system for planning instruction based on assessing the needs and strengths of the students, provides both strategies for comprehension and developing content products. In a series of research studies

(O'Malley, Chamot, Stewner-Manzanares, Russo, & Kipper, 1985a, 1985b; O'Malley, Chamot, & Kupper, 1989), the two primary authors established that successful ESL students utilized a series of strategies to help themselves through English texts. Chamot and O'Malley categorized these strategies as metacognitive, cognitive, and social/affective. They determined how the strategies operated within each particular content area, and what bodies of declarative and procedural knowledge students would need to comprehend the important concepts and skills for each content area. Declarative knowledge refers to the content knowledge itself, like the issues surrounding the American Revolution, whereas procedural knowledge refers to processes, such as the scientific process in science or the research process in language arts or social studies (Chamot & O'Malley, 1994).

They then studied a number of instructional concepts based on cognitive models of learning (Chamot & O'Malley, 1986), and selected their most appropriate features to form CALLA. These instructional concepts are: Language Across the Curriculum; the Language Experience Approach; Whole Language; Process Writing; Cooperative Learning; and Cognitive Instruction (Chamot & O'Malley, 1994). An important part of the ultimate lesson structure was the use of assessment throughout the lesson, beginning with a comprehensive examination of what the learners already knew about the topic and which strategies they used regularly to access texts. This insured that teachers would not just design a plan that would be redundant or too basic for the students. Finally, Chamot and O'Malley devised a lesson structure to include three kinds of learning objectives: content; academic language and processes and learning strategies. Using these three learning objectives as a base, teachers could design instruction and create learning contexts that would move students toward grade-appropriate content literacy.

Becoming Critical Content Teachers

As noted earlier, I teach language arts and reading instruction in a bilingual credential program. The primary objective in my content area reading methods course for middle school and high school pre-service teachers is to help them become the thorough, linguistically knowledgeable, and critically conscious content instructors their non-mainstream students will need. Nevertheless, it is not surprising that my students begin the course with the idea that they will be teaching only their content--science, math, social science, literature--because they have had limited models for teaching their content areas in other than traditional ways. They are shocked to realize that they are as responsible for language and reading development as are English as Second Language, sheltered, and mainstream English teachers. However, after introducing them to lists that focus along the same lines as the one below on each of their content areas, they begin to understand why they must incorporate language and reading skills within their content lessons:

What's Difficult About Social Studies for ESL Students?

- Curriculum assumes prior historical, geographical, and civic knowledge and culturally based values which may be unfamiliar to students.
- Specialized vocabulary often refers to abstract concepts.
- Discourse is primarily expository; language functions include both lower and higher-level thinking skills.
- Reading texts include sentences with multiple embedded clauses, complex past tense forms, and extensive use of pronouns.
- Decontextualized language is used in relationship to unfamiliar concepts.
- Students may have had little experience locating information, using maps and graphs, and using effective strategies for listening, reading, and writing (Chamot & O'Malley, 1994, p. 263).

To make the point more effectively, I ask them to bring middle school or high school textbooks in their content areas on the day I present the lists. After they have reflected upon and discussed the lists in content-alike groups, I ask them to analyze several randomly chosen passages from the textbooks using the lists as their lens. Invariably, students in all the content areas realize how difficult the texts are when there is a lack of an appropriate academic language and process knowledge base.

The pre-service teachers are also mystified by the need to introduce and practice metacognitive, cognitive, and social/affective strategies in addition to the content, because they themselves use these strategies at a level so automatic that they think all people know how to use them. The best way I have found to explain the importance of such strategies is to compare the strategies as the key to a large building that contains many offices. Having a key to one office is useless if they don't have the key to open the building itself. They must have one to use the other. Over the course of the semester, my students produce and teach five or six lessons that include the introduction and practice of various metacognitive, cognitive, and social/affective strategies. Through these experiences, they realize how essential the strategies are to the comprehension of content, and they become convinced. Their final project is a ten-day thematic unit that uses the CALLA lesson characteristics. It is important to note that these characteristics support the principles of status equalization and codes of power found in my research study (Table 1). The CALLA lessons are academically rigorous because they must be aligned with grade level content standards and state frameworks, yet are comprehensible to second language students because the CALLA structure offers so much scaffolding. An instructor can develop learning units that support students to critically engage course content with their worlds. The use of prior knowledge and the real-life applications of content explicitly call for the teacher and students to connect the topic of study with meaningful lived experiences of the students and conditions in the community. For example, the thematic units produced for the course included such topics as: "Does Homelessness Equate to Helplessness?"--this was a social studies unit that explored the economic picture during the Depression and compared it to economics of the 1990's; "The More Things Change, the More Things Stay the Same"; "The Civil Rights Movement: How Did It Impact Our Lives Today?" Other thematic units were collaborations between two or more subject teachers. One of these explored the effect of "El Niño" through science, math, social studies, and language arts. Another studied the Manhattan Project through science, social studies, language arts, and physical /health education (What are the physical effects of radiation? was a question explored within that subject).

Another component in a CALLA lesson is student self-evaluation, which enables students to develop autonomy and a better sense of individual strengths and weaknesses that can help them study more productively. This component was especially intriguing to my students because they never had teachers who encouraged them to become their own evaluators at the middle or high school level. The students had unquestioningly "bought into" the notion of evaluation as a unilateral part of teaching and learning. The inclusion of devices by which their students could examine their own learning was one of the high points of the pre-service teachers' instructional repertoire.

Uncritical Uses of Learning Strategies

It would be much simpler to present the CALLA merely as a functional, practical template for teaching to my students. However, it is important for them to understand that any strategies, formats, devices, or plans they are likely to encounter have the potential for both good and poor teaching. This is where the notion of critical educator comes into play. For example, uncritical, across-the-board use of learning aids like anticipation guides each and every time students read their texts denotes a teacher who does not plan instruction based on observation and assessment of his students. Instruction that does not fit the needs and strengths of students creates frustration in those for whom such scaffolding actually hinders their engagement with text.

The over-use and mis-use of cooperative learning is another example. It is too often the case that teachers who have not had in-depth training in heterogeneous grouping of students for the purpose of learning content will allow abuses such as "hitch-hiking," a term that describes one student in a group doing all the cognitive work, while the rest participate in minimal ways but receive the same grade as the lone worker. Teachers who organize their students to superficially resemble cooperative groups because this "looks" like culturally-sensitive pedagogy are cheating all of the students in the class. I want to acknowledge that during my presentation of the material in this paper, members of the audience described a number of classroom environments, including the two above, that used some strategies proposed by CALLA, but were poorly applied. It is clear that these were examples of the uncritical use of potentially empowering learning scaffolds. In summary, even well-conceived instructional structures with the potential for liberatory teaching and learning can be used in oppressive ways.

**Beyond Academic Language: Creating the Conditions
for the Voices of Difference**

I have gone into considerable detail here on how I drive the point home to pre-service teachers about the need to establish the development of academic language and processes. But even this is not enough to assure that non-mainstream students will use their gains in learning to move beyond functional literacy. Our goal should not be satisfied through our students' mastery of complex literate discourses. We must also nurture students' voices in their expression of insights gained through critical analyses of their personal and community realities, which they can learn to conduct through our critical teaching practices. This brings us to yet another stage; through our help, our students must learn to use the language of theory (Darder, 1991). They must be free to develop their bicultural voices among members of their own learning communites—our classrooms—and the home communities beyond the school walls. Ultimately

> ...it is also imperative that, in order to understand more fully the impact of language on social structures and practices, students of color enter into critical dialogues with those outside their cultural communities. Through the process of these cross-cultural dialogues, these students come to better recognize for themselves the manner in which language works to define who they are, and how language as a tool can assist them to explore critically those possibilities that have remained hidden and out of their reach (Darder, 1991, p. 104).

And it all begins with developing mainstream discourse skills, but with a critical consciousness!

References

Chamot, A. U., and O'Malley, J. M. (1994). *The CALLA Handbook: Implementing the Cognitive Academic Language Learning Approach.* Reading, MA: Addison-Wesley.
_____. (1986). *A Cognitive Academic Language Approach: An ESL Content-Based Curriculum.* Rosslyn, VA: National Clearinghouse for Bilingual Education.

Cummins, J. (1979). "Cognitive Academic Language Proficiency, Linguistic Interdependence, Optimal Age and Some Other Matters." *Working papers on Bilingualism*, 19, pp. 197-205.

Darder, A. (1991). *Culture and Power in the Classroom: A Critical Foundation for Bicultural Education.* NY: Bergin & Garvey.

Delpit, L. (1995). *Other People's Children: Cultural Conflict in the Classroom.* NY: The New Press.

_____. (1988). "The Silenced Dialogue: Power and Pedagogy in Educating Other People's Children." *Harvard Educational Review*, 58 (3), pp. 280-298.

Fordham, S. (1988). "Racelessness as a Factor in Black Students' Success: Pragmatic Strategy or Pyrrhic Victory?" *Harvard Educational Review*, 58 (1), pp. 29-84.

Gee, J. P. (1991). "What is Literacy?" In C. Mitchell & K. Weiler (Eds.). *Rewriting Literacy: Culture and the Discourse of the Other.* NY: Bergin & Garvey, pp. 3-11.

Hollins, E. R. (1996). *Culture in School Learning: Revealing the Deep Meaning.* Mahweh, NJ: Lawrence Erlbaum Publisher.

Jones, E. B. (1998). Mexican American Teachers as Cultural Mediators: Literacy and literacy contexts through bicultural strengths. Unpublished dissertation. Claremont, CA and San Diego, CA: Claremont Graduate University and San Diego State University.

Macedo, D. (1991). "The politics of an Emancipatory Literacy in Cape Verde." In C. Mitchell, and K. Weiler (Eds.). *Rewriting Literacy: Culture and the Discourse of the Other.* NY: Bergin & Garvey, pp. 147-159.

O'Malley, J. M., Chamot, A. U., and Kupper, L. (1989). "Listening Comprehension Strategies in Second Language Acquisition." *Applied Linguistics*, 10 (4).

O'Malley, J. M., Chamot, A. U., Stewner-Manzanares, G., Russo, R. P., and Kupper, L. (1985a). "Learning Strategies Used by Beginning and Intermediate ESL Students." *Language Learning*, 35, pp. 21-46.

_____. (1985b). "Learning Strategy Applications with Students of English as a Second Language." *TESOL Quarterly*, 19, pp. 285-296.

Peregoy, S. F., and Boyle, O. F. (1997). *Reading, Writing, & Learning in ESL: A Resource Book for K-12 Teachers, 2nd Ed.* NY: Longman.

Shannon, P. (1990). *The Struggle to Continue: Progressive Reading Instruction in the United States.* Portsmouth, NH: Heinemann.

Valdés, G. (1994). "English Con Salsa." In L. M. Carlson (Ed.). *Cool Salsa: Bilingual Poems on Growing Up in the United States.* NY: Fawcett Juniper, pp. 3-4.

LEARNING TOGETHER: ASL-ENGLISH BILINGUAL-BICULTURAL EARLY CHILDHOOD CLASSROOM

Bobbie M. Allen

In the United States, bilingual education for deaf children has been discussed for the past 20 years. Nevertheless, educators, administrators and families are just beginning to recognize bilingual practices as innovative and a possible avenue for educating deaf and hard of hearing children. Even though there is growing support from some educators, administrators and families, there remain questions and skepticism from others. The questions, skepticism and resistance to implementation of bilingual practices is partly due to: (a) the culture and power struggles in the field for well over 100 years, (b) the language status of American Sign Language (ASL), (c) the two different modalities in which English and ASL are represented, and (d) the narrow focus in the field with regard to teaching practices and strategies that have been used in classrooms for deaf and hard of hearing children.

From past research, there has been evidence that traditional programs, Oral/Aural and Total Communication (TC) classrooms where teachers use oral English or manually coded English (MCE) systems for instruction, have not provided a complete language model for deaf and hard of hearing children (Johnson, Liddell, & Erting, 1989; Kluwin, 1981; Marmor & Petitto, 1979). In essence, the children have not developed the necessary tools to access the English language and achieve academically (Bowe, 1991; COED, 1988). Additionally, research has clearly provided evidence that deaf children are not equal to their hearing counterparts in academic achievement. In fact, the average reading level of a deaf high school graduate has been between a 3rd and 4th grade (Bowe, 1991; COED, 1988).

Traditional teaching practices that continue to oppress deaf and hard of hearing children and their families need to be re-evaluated, and a restructuring needs to occur in deaf education. Traditional values and practices that allow only a few deaf children to be successful within the academic setting need to be discarded and replaced with effective practices that foster success for the majority. Johnson, Liddell & Erting (1989) highlighted the fact that deaf education has failed in spite of the fact that class sizes are small compared to their hearing counterparts (eight to ten is typical), teachers are highly trained specialists and typically hold an MA or MEd degrees, and the cost of educating a deaf child is quite high when compared to that of educating hearing children in the public schools. They posed the question: "How is it possible that such a well-developed, costly, and elaborate system has failed?" (p. 3). According to these researchers, there are two primary reasons for the failure of deaf education: (1) lack of linguistic access to curricular content, and (2) low expectations of deaf children (p. 3).

Deaf children do not acquire spoken languages in the same manner as hearing children, primarily for the obvious reason: they can not perceive the spoken language in the same manner as hearing children. Even with hearing aids and cochlear implants, the sounds are different and distorted and do not raise the level of hearing to that of a hearing person. Every child's experience is different with each of these devices. Some children are more successful than others in finding ways to use the devices to access the English language in both spoken and written texts. The author is certainly not advocating that these devices not be included in the education of deaf children, but it is critical that families be provided all of the information and the perspectives of both the deaf and hearing worlds. Well-intentioned medical professionals and the educational community (typically hearing individuals, not deaf) often mislead parents and children into thinking that their children will and must grow up and "talk" like hearing people. There is little mention of how difficult that might be for the children and their families and the impact it may have on the children's academic achievement.

Often, families are discouraged from using sign language with their children in fear that it will inhibit the children's ability to learn the English language; research, however, has disproved this (Gardner & Zorfass, 1983). In fact, Hatfield, Caccamise, and Siple (1978) found that ASL actually promoted rather than inhibited or impeded the acquisition of English. Hearing families are not prepared when they do learn that their children are deaf. As a result, the families are confronted with a staggering amount of information and often feel guilty because they feel unprepared to make the right decisions. They often become confused by the claims and counterclaims of what is educationally sound for their deaf children and very fearful of what the future holds for their children (Lane, Hoffmeister & Bahan, 1996, pp. 35-36). The abundance of information to families, exclusive of that from the deaf community, continues to perpetuate the strained relationships between the hearing world and the deaf community.

Furthermore, teachers' views and identification with the dominant culture and traditional pedagogy can influence the families, can delay the enculturation process for the children in their classrooms, and alienate the deaf community from the educational community and families. Thus, when teachers and classrooms are only aligned with the dominant culture (hearing) and ignore the subordinate culture(s) (deaf and other minorities) the outcome for families and their children can potentially be very negative. Under these conditions, the emphasis is primarily on the children's deficits based on the standards of the dominant culture. Conversely, when families are given information about the deaf community, they are essentially provided with a life-long resource and a network of people who can help facilitate their children's linguistic, social, emotional and cognitive development (Lane, Hoffmeister & Bahan, 1996; Mahshie, 1995; Allen, 1998).

As opposed to the experiences of hearing families, deaf families often celebrate their children's deafness (Erting, 1985; Lane, Hoffmeister & Bahan, 1996). The children in deaf families are treated like any other children in that the expectations and opportunities for these children to function in both deaf and hearing worlds is rarely questioned. This fact has been recognized as a contributing factor in deaf children of deaf families outperforming deaf children of hearing families on most academic measures (Corson, 1973). Within deaf families, children have opportunities to develop in very natural, spontaneous and normal ways without any setbacks, especially where the environment provides a naturally accessible language (Corson, 1973; Erting, 1985; Lane, Hoffmeister & Bahan, 1996).

One of the most critical issues in deaf education today is how to foster language and literacy development in order to increase the academic achievement of deaf and hard of hearing students. Information and research findings have led to the importance of early childhood programs and their approaches to facilitating early literacy and language development in both English and ASL. Just adding ASL to the classroom environment will not be sufficient to change how deaf and hard of hearing children succeed in the educational setting. Materials, methods, and a strong curriculum combined with high expectations need to be included as a way to promote bilingual/bicultural practices in the classroom. Additionally, well-designed bilingual classrooms need to be supported as equally viable options for the education of deaf and hard of hearing children, as are the other options that are currently available.

Despite the resistance to implementing ASL-English bilingual practices, a team of teachers in a large urban school district in southern California is implementing innovative practices and currently influencing others to change classroom environments. These teachers are developing teaching methods in an effort to find effective ways to educate young deaf and hard of hearing children bilingually. Their classroom was selected as an exemplar program by the state of California which allows them to act as consultants. Additionally, site visitations to their classroom are provided for those who are interested in setting up similar classrooms in their own school districts in California and out of the state.

Traditional teacher education programs had trained the team of teachers in this early childhood classroom; that is, their training focused on the medical perspective rather than the cultural perspective. From their many years of teaching deaf and hard of hearing children in Oral/Aural and Total Communication classrooms, the team of teachers realized the ineffectiveness of such practices. Through their own research efforts and the desire to see deaf and hard of hearing children succeed, they designed a classroom based on bilingual principles and practices. They critically examined their own traditional values and beliefs and replaced them with transformed values and beliefs that challenged the status quo.

A combination of bilingual teaching practices and daily reflection on those practices created a classroom that was forever changing the lives of deaf, hard of hearing, hearing children and their families who observed and participated within the classroom. In essence, the teachers provided a rich communicative environment that facilitated the deaf, hard of hearing and hearing children's learning. They became facilitators and created a classroom that was child-centered rather than teacher-centered. They were also successful in creating a strong community through their interactions with the families and the deaf community. They were continually seeking ways of assessing the children that were appropriate for very young deaf, hard of hearing and hearing children. Thus, they adopted an additive approach, rather than a subtractive, providing a guiding framework for restructuring their classroom for deaf and hard of hearing children.

The ASL-English bilingual/bicultural classroom is unique for children who are deaf, hard of hearing and hearing and under the age of five. The enrollment of carefully selected hearing children from families using ASL and English in the home allowed for larger class size and multi-age groupings. Traditional educators criticized these two aspects of the classroom, but they were crucial for the success of the children. An increased class size combined with the multi-age setting had several benefits. First, they allowed the children to have many peers from whom to choose for interaction, regardless of their language or language ability. Second, the children were able to cross cultural and linguistic boundaries through their interactions with their peers and the adults, thereby providing an environment that supported access to information and conversations in ASL and English. Third, there was easy and free-flowing communication among deaf, hard of hearing and hearing peers, as well as with the adults. Fourth, it provided a critical mass of language peers for deaf and hard of hearing children. Fifth, the older peers became excellent role models for the younger children creating an environment whereby the younger children learned from their older classmates. Sixth, the increased class size contributed to the development of an effective program incorporating innovative teaching practices that were typically used in general education, early childhood programs, as well as bilingual programs.

With a smaller class size, as has been the case in traditional classrooms, many teaching practices had been difficult to implement. Additionally, traditional settings have made it difficult to create a rich communicative environment because there were so few children and adult language models. Finally, the large class size helped reduce the tendency of the teachers to "be in control." With a larger class size, the teacher could not systematically control every activity. Of course, there was structure, and goals for each activity, but it was neither logical nor practical to try to force the children to sit for long periods of time at a u-shaped table waiting for each child to respond to the teacher. The teachers carefully explained the activities and routines and the children were expected to follow the established rules. The children, therefore, had a choice of which learning activities they wanted to do, as well as with whom they would choose to participate.

Bringing young deaf, hard of hearing and hearing children together who could share ideas and learn through a common language while striving for bilingualism, seemed like a very simple idea and a way to achieve successful integration. The design and implementation of this two-way bilingual model adapted for deaf, hard of hearing and hearing children proved to be effective for most of the children. The teachers designed an environment wherein the children felt safe and were willing to take risks. The rich communicative environment provided each child an avenue for acquiring two languages, ASL and English, without feeling forced to use only one language that may or may not have been his/her most comfortable mode of communication. In essence, the children's communication was easy and free flowing. They were engaged in a variety of activities with a diverse group of peers and were able to make choices in their learning. The choice factor and the themes and hands-on activities that revolved around carefully selected children's books made the classroom highly motivating for the children.

As suggested earlier, deafness not only impacts the life of a child, but the entire family. The families who had children enrolled in this classroom began to understand the benefits of their children becoming bilingual/bicultural early on; that is, "fluent communication, positive self-image, and a basis for English mastery"(Lane, Hoffmeister, & Bahan, 1996, p. 300). They also viewed their children as bilingual learners rather than "broken" children who needed to be fixed in order to be like a hearing person. Without the team of teachers and their efforts to change their classroom, these families would not have understood the benefits of bilingualism nor would they have developed sensitivity towards the deaf community, the culture and ASL.

As a result, several of the English-dominant families were able to closely align themselves with the deaf community through the collaborative efforts of the teachers and the teachers' sensitivity to the cultures represented in their classroom. The teachers understood the importance of the families being exposed to deaf role models, deaf culture and ASL. This contributed to the families becoming strong in their belief that their deaf and hard of hearing children could succeed. The teachers bridged the gap between the two cultures to help the families understand the similarities and differences of both cultures. Strained relationships between hearing and deaf people in this classroom became an issue of the past. Helping each other to raise their children and to respect each other's culture and language became the underlying principles that were guiding many of these families. It was a critical aspect of the program that helped facilitate the children's overall development, built a strong community within the classroom, and later, unified actions of all the families and the deaf community to deter the school district's attempts to disband or change the program. It appears that a new paradigm for deaf education within this public school setting emerged.

In this classroom, the storybooks that were selected by the teachers for story time became the children's favorite storybooks. For some children, the classroom experience with storytelling was their first. Many of the hearing families looked at books with their children, but were still struggling at home in telling a complete story using ASL. Therefore, this became a critical time of day for the children's exposure to books and stories. After the teachers told the story in ASL and English, being careful to separate the languages, the children had the opportunity to share the same book that was just presented with each other and adults during book sharing time. The book sharing time provided the children with a time to experience extensive interaction with adults and their peers discussing books and stories. Often, these same books were selected by the children to be read during other times of the day. Their emergent reading behaviors were noted and documented when they were engaged with their "favorite" books used for story time and book sharing as well as unfamiliar books they chose during guided play. Two tools, *The California Learning Record* (Barr & Syverson, 1994) and the *Nonverbal and Verbal Emergent Reading Behaviors Observational Checklist* (Allen, 1998) helped identify, describe and categorize the deaf and hard of hearing children's emergent reading behaviors.

The children's cognitive development was also very significant. The cognitive development of the children played a key role in how they: (a) solved problems on their own, (b) understood the stories presented during storytelling and then retold the stories to their peers and adults, (c) developed a metalinguistic awareness of the two languages present in the classroom, (d) conversed about a variety of topics in a very natural and spontaneous manner, and (e) used finger spelling, writing, reading and the interchange of signed and spoken languages while engaged in literacy activities. It was clear that the use and interaction of the two languages, ASL and English, contributed to their cognitive development. Ultimately, the development in these two areas, language and cognition, are critical for their future success in the academic setting. A closer look at George will help further one's understanding of how deaf children develop literacy at a very young age when provided a restructured environment that empowers children and families.

When George was first observed in the classroom, he was 3:11 years old. The term "reading" has been used rather loosely when describing George's emergent reading behaviors. Although he was not actually "reading" the printed text, he appeared to be reading and was very engaged in each book that he chose. Because of the tremendous exposure to books and storytelling in the classroom and in the home, it was clear that George was "becoming a reader" based on how he interacted with books and print.

George displayed a love for books and telling stories in both the home and school settings. While his retelling of the stories was picture-governed, there were strong indications that he was moving to actually reading the text. He had a solid understanding of the development of a story and used the pictures to "read" the story alone and when he retold the story to others. He also had an understanding that the printed text had meaning. He had made the connection that there was a one-to-one correspondence between the hand shapes in finger spelling and the printed letters. This was evidenced by his attempts to finger spell titles of books, objects and names of people, as well as his own name. He was observed using his index finger to "track" the text on the page. Overall, he had a very good sense of the components of a story and told the story using ASL to his friends, interested adults and his family. After he gained confidence in the understanding of the story, he was quick to interact and share with others what he knew. He enjoyed "reading" the books that were selected for storytelling time by the teachers. His favorite books at the time included, but were not limited to: *Stella Luna, Little Lumpty, A Tent Too Full, Where's My Teddy?, The Three Pigs, The Three Bears,* and *Little Miss Muffet.*

George demonstrated a pattern when "reading" the stories that were just presented by the teachers. During book sharing time, he was often observed very engaged with the book, reading and looking at each page and the pictures carefully prior to interacting and sharing with his friends about the story. He preferred to thoroughly look at the book alone, then share it with an adult and, finally, with his friends. The way George interacted with books can best be described through an incident that happened one day during book sharing of the story Little Miss Muffet. After he completely perused the story of Little Miss Muffet alone, he signed to the teacher that he wanted to eat. She reassured him that it was almost snack time. Satisfied with the answer, he then started looking at the book again page by page. He tapped one of his younger deaf friends, Brady, on the shoulder to try to get him to turn to the same page and look at the same picture. His friend was not too cooperative. Nevertheless, George consistently tried to persuade his friend to look at the same page by tapping his friend for his attention and pointing at the picture in his book and then in Brady's book. Brady became somewhat irritated with George's persistent and bothersome behavior and turned away from him. George then turned his attention back to his own book.

George noticed the teacher and other children sharing the book. As the other children began to discuss the book with the teacher, George decided to get involved with the group. After a few minutes with the group, he stood up and casually dropped his book to the floor and proceeded to wash his hands to get ready for morning snacks. Afterwards, he returned to the book sharing circle and picked up the book again. He examined the title page of the book for a few moments. He then attempted to finger spell the title of the book, letter by letter. He carefully finger spelled and touched each letter printed on the page with approximations and some appropriate hand shapes. The teacher noticed and quickly sat down to facilitate his finger spelling. While the teacher was helping George, Brady who had been sitting next to George and watching very closely, tapped the teacher to get her attention. He, too, wanted to demonstrate his skills in finger spelling the title.

It was most intriguing for the author to watch George interact with the illustrations in the books. It was as if each picture came alive for him. He noticed the smallest details and then attempted to explain what was happening, or created his own story. During book sharing of *Pumpkin Time*, George sat near Judy, the teacher, and constantly tapped her to get her attention, commenting or retelling the story as he turned each page of the book. With each illustration he also gave a clear description. For example, George pointed to each little seed depicted on the page. To indicate the growth of the seedlings, he would start signing "grow" directly on top of each seedling represented on the page. He inflected the sign "grow" to emphasize how the seedlings quickly grew into small plants. He continued on a later page showing the slow and gradual growth into a vine. Later, he used the descriptive classifier, CL:G, to quantify the size of the tiny pumpkins growing on the vine. He even held his "g" hand up to his eye, squinting, to further emphasize the miniature size of the pumpkin.

George's ability to describe the pictures and retell stories was not only observed during book sharing times with familiar books that had just been presented to the class, but also with unfamiliar books during other times of the day. One day, during guided play, he found an informational book about snakes. The book was rather tattered and worn, but the pictures intrigued George. He was fascinated by the life cycle of the snake. He took the book to the teacher, who was sitting in the kitchen/housekeeping area, and began discussing the pictures with her. There were other children in the area and they, too, became fascinated by the information in the book. Before long, there was plenty of conversation among the group of children about snakes. There was a tremendous amount of learning about snakes happening for all the children involved. The teacher served as a facilitator and the children's resource when there was a question that needed to be answered about the snakes.

Afterwards, George was seen looking at the snake book alone and engaged with one particular picture in the snake book. The illustration was a nest full of snake eggs. At first, George tried to scoop up the eggs with both hands, and then, meticulously picked up each imaginary egg and placed it in the palm of his hand. He gazed at the imaginary eggs in his palm for a few moments, and suddenly, slammed his hand down on the table. He lifted his hand from the table and looked at his hand in disgust. He proceeded to pick off part of the imaginary eggshells from his palm. Imagining that his hands were very dirty, he walked to the sink to wash his hands. This particular incident demonstrated George's fantastic imagination and his ability to create stories from the illustrations. He had an extraordinary way of interacting with the pictures and then expressing what he saw either through expressive language (ASL) or through his actions using mime and gestures.

George had a tremendous exposure to books in the classroom and at home. The family's nightly story time combined with the classroom story time and book sharing facilitated his understanding that books have interesting information and stories are meaningful and fun. His book handling skills demonstrated his understanding that the books had a purpose and were not just play items. He went through each book carefully, familiar and unfamiliar, page by page as if he were reading the text. His re-enactment of the stories was still closely tied to the pictures as described in Sulzby's (1985) classification scheme, and must therefore be considered "Picture-Governed Attempts." His stories, however, appeared to be moving toward "Print-Governed Attempts" based on his finger spelling of certain words in the text. He began to track full sentences on the pages with his index finger. His reenactments of the stories became more complex, evidenced by his use of various ASL structures to describe in detail the aspects of each illustration on each page and the cohesiveness of the story across the pages. He no longer randomly turned the pages to label, compare or follow the action of the illustrations. His ASL storytelling strategies increased in complexity as evidenced by his use of role shifting and assuming the role of characters to help identify the various characters in the story. Other children in this classroom developed in similar ways which strongly suggests that the redesigned classroom combined with bilingual teaching practices and high expectations for the children have influenced the development of the deaf, hard of hearing and hearing children as well as their families.

In conclusion, the words of Paulo Friere (1990) seem most appropriate when considering the history of deaf education, the failure of so many deaf children, and the emergence of a new paradigm: "The solution is not to integrate them into the structure of oppression, but to transform that structure so that they can become beings for themselves."

The classroom examined above has done just that: transformed the structure for the children and their families; they are empowered and making new paths for others to follow. These families have found that they do have a voice in the education of their children, and as the years go by the children will discover that they have a voice in their schools and in their communities. Together, these children, families, and teachers will change the education of deaf children in order that a new paradigm be embraced, a paradigm of equity, equality and excellence that empowers the voice of deaf and hard of hearing children as well as their families.

References

Allen, B. M. (1998). ASL-English Bilingual-Bicultural Early Childhood Classroom: Deaf Children and the Families' Perspectives. Dissertation Abstracts International, vol. 59-018, UMI.

_____. (1998). "Nonverbal and Verbal Emergent Reading Behaviors Observational Checklist," in B.M. Allen, *ASL-English Bilingual-Bicultural Early Childhood Classroom: Deaf Children and the Families' Perspectives.* Dissertation Abstracts International, v. 59-018, UMI.

Barr, M. A., Syverson, M. A. (1994). *California Learning Record (CLR).* El Cajon, CA: Center for Language Learning.

Bowe, F. (1991). *Approaching Equality: Education of the Deaf.* Silver Spring, MD: T.J. Publishers.

Commission on Education of the Deaf (COED). (1988). *Toward Equality: Education of the Deaf.* Washington, D.C.: U.S. Government.

Corson, H. (1973). Comparing deaf children of oral deaf parents and deaf parents using manual communication with deaf children of hearing parents on academic, social and communicative functioning. Unpublished doctoral dissertation, University of Cincinnati.

Erting, C. (1994). *Deafness, Communication, Social Identity: Ethnography in a Preschool for Deaf Children.* Burtonsville, MD: Linstok Press.

Friere, P. (1990). *The Pedagogy of the Oppressed.* NY: Seabury Press.

Gardner, J., and Zorfass, J. (1983). "From Sign to Speech: The Language Development of a Hearing Impaired Child." *American Annals of the Deaf*, pp. 20-31.

Hattfield, N., Caccamise, F., and Siple, P. (1978). "Deaf Students Language Competency: A Bilingual Perspective." *American Annals of the Deaf*, 123, pp. 847-851.

Johnson, R. E., Liddell, S. K., and Erting, C. J. (1989). *Unlocking the Curriculum: Principles for Achieving Access in Deaf Education.* Washington, D.C.: Department of Linguistics and Interpreting and Gallaudet Research Institute.

Kluwin, T. (1981). "A Rationale for Modifying Classroom Signing Systems." *Sign Language Studies,* 31, pp. 179-187.

Lane, H., Hoffmeister, R., and Bahan, B. (1996). *A Journey into the Deaf-World.* San Diego, CA: DawnSignPress.

Mahshie, S. N. 1995). *Educating Deaf Children Bilingually.* Washington, D.C.: Pre-College Programs, Gallaudet University.

Marmor, G., and Pettito, L. (1979). "Simultaneous Communication in the Classroom: How Well is Grammar Represented?" *Sign Language Studies*, 23, pp. 99-136.

Sulzby, E. (1985). "Children's Emergent Reading of Favorite Storybooks: A Developmental Study." *Reading Research Quarterly*, 20, pp. 458-481.

BOOK LINKS: CONNECTING LITERATURE AND THE CURRICULUM

Carolyn Angus & Nancy Brashear

In developing our "Book Links" list, we have read widely among recently published children's books and selected books that are good choices for both reading aloud and reading alone. You can also link many of the books in our "Book Links" list to your curriculum.

Begin With Mother Goose: Nursery Rhymes & Songs. Here are our favorites of the new collections of nursery rhymes and songs and single-rhyme picture book editions. These well-loved verses are good introductions to children's literary heritage. They also serve to build a sense of the rhythms of language and help to develop vocabulary and auditory memory.

Iona Opie's *My Very First Mother Goose* and the *My Very First Mother Goose Board Books* series
Simms Taback's *There was an Old Lady who Swallowed a Fly*
Shari Halpern's *Hush, Little Baby*
Lullabies: An Illustrated Songbook

Poetry, Please. Include poetry in your read-aloud sessions. Read poems and reread favorites every day. We have selected collections of poems noteworthy for their imaginative and beautiful language and thought-provoking content as well as some light, playful verses.

Jack Prelutsky's *The Beauty of the Beast: Poems from the Animal Kingdom*
Douglas Florian's *Insectlopedia*
Kristine O'Connell George's *The Great Frog Race and Other Poems*
In Daddy's Arms I Am Tall: African Americans Celebrating Fathers
Paul Janeczko's *That Sweet Diamond: Baseball Poems*
I Am Writing a Poem About...: A Game of Poetry edited by Myra Cohn Livingston

<u>Some Perfect Pairs</u>. Read pairs of picture books, a picture book and a related nonfiction book, a poem and a nonfiction or picture book, or folktales that are linked in some way.

Kate Banks' *And If the Moon Could Talk* and Margaret Wise Brown's
 Goodnight Moon
Karen Beaumont Alarcón's *Louella Mae, She's Run Away!* and Lynn
 Plourde's *Pigs in the Mud in the Middle of the Rud*
Marc Simont's *The Goose That Almost Got Cooked* and Jan Wahl's *The
 Singing Geese*
Pat Mora's *Tomás and the Library Lady* and William Miller's *Richard
 Wright and the Library Card*
Make Things Fly: Poems About the Wind edited by Dorothy M.
 Kennedy and Brian G. Karas' *The Windy Day*
Richard Egielski's *The Gingerbread Boy* and Mirra Ginsburg's *Clay Boy*
Jan Peck's *The Giant Carrot* and Vladimir Vagin's *The Enormous
 Carrot*
Susan Lowell's *Little Red Cowboy Hat* and a traditional retelling of *Little
 Red Riding Hood*
James Berry's *First Palm Trees: An Anancy Spiderman Story* and Nancy
 Van Laan's *The Magic Bean Tree: A Legend from Argentina*

<u>It's Just As Good As—Or Better Than Or Almost As Good As—The
First Book</u>! Read aloud a sequel or the latest book in a series. Children will turn to the earlier books for reading on their own.

Janet Morgan Stoeke's *A Friend for Minerva Louise*
Rosemary Wells' *Bunny Cakes* and *Bunny Money*
Betsy Byars' *Ant Plays Bear*
Sylvia Waugh's *Mennyms Alive*

<u>I Have A Tale To Tell</u>. Make folktales and legends a part of your read-aloud sessions. We have included some new picture book editions of old favorites as well as collections.

Paul O. Zelinsky's *Rapunzel*
Virginia Hamilton's *A Ring of Tricksters: Animal Tales from America,
 the West Indies, and Africa*

Nancy Van Laan's *With a Whoop and a Holler: A Bushel of Lore from
    Way Down South*
John Bierhorst's *The Dancing Fox: Arctic Folktales*
Mary Pope Osborne's *Favorite Medieval Tales*
Una Leavy's *Irish Fairy Tales and Legends*
Neil Philip's *Fairy Tales of the Brothers Grimm*

Picture Books. Here are a few of our favorite new picture books that
make good read alouds. Children will want to hear these stories again
and again or to read them on their own, after you have read them aloud.

Linnea Riley's *Mouse Mess*
Rhonda Gowler Greene's *Barnyard Song*
Elizabeth MacDonald's *The Wolf Is Coming!*
Kate Duke's *One Guinea Pig Is Not Enough*
Shen Roddie's *Too Close Friends*
Erica Silverman's *On the Morn of Mayfest*

Easy-to-Read Book. Few books in an easy-to-read format for beginning
readers make good read alouds. Here are two that do. You'll also want
to have earlier books in these series available for children to read and
reread independently.

Cynthia Rylant's *Henry and Mudge and the Sneaky Crackers*
Cynthia Rylant's *Mr. Putter and Tabby Toot the Horn*

Information to Go. Here are some informational books that make good
read-aloud fare. These can also be used to introduce themes of study and
for enriching textbook content.

Nicola Davies' *Big Blue Whale*
Sandra and William Markle's *Gone Forever!: An Alphabet of Extinct
    Animals*
Ken Mochizuki's *Passage to Freedom: The Sugihara Story*
Don Brown's *Alice Ramsey's Grand Adventure*
Dr. Martin Luther King, Jr.'s *I Have a Dream*

Old Favorites in New Editions. Use the publication of new editions to
introduce children to old favorites.

Arnold Lobel's *The Arnold Lobel Book of Mother Goose*
Rosemary Wells' *Max and Ruby* board books
Rosemary Wells' *Noisy Nora*
Leo Lionni's *Frederick's Fables*
Jerry Pinkney's *Rikki-tikki-tavi*
Ruth Stiles Gannett's *Three Tales of My Father's Dragon*

A Bibliography of Read-Aloud/Read-Alone Books
Compiled by Carolyn Angus

Alarcón, Karen Beaumont. (1997). *Louella Mae, She's Run Away!*
    Illus. by Rosanne Litzinger. New York: Holt.
"Louella Mae, she's run away!" Everyone on the farm is searching for her high and low. As night falls the weary and forlorn searchers return to the house—and discover Louella Mae snug in a tub with (as the final double-page illustration shows) her five newborn piglets. (Picture book)

Banks, Kate. (1998). *And if the Moon Could Talk.* Illus. by Georg
    Hallensleben. New York: Farrar.
It's bedtime "and if the moon could talk" it could tell of the things it looks down on all over the world (scenes related to various toys and objects in a child's room) and say good night to "a child curled up in bed wrapped in sleep." (Picture book)

Berry, James. (1997). *First Palm Trees: An Anancy Spiderman Story.*
    Illus. by Greg Couch. New York: Simon & Schuster.
In this tales from the West Indies, Anancy Spiderman seeks the rich reward the king promises to give the individual who makes the priest's dream of a new kind of tree come true. Berry's writing is rhythmic and rich in repetitive patterns. Couch's portrayal of Anancy plays up the trickster's spidery aspects: long legs and multiple eyes (sunglasses, round glasses, and reading glasses worn at the same time). (Folklore)

Bierhorst, John (Ed.). (1997). *The Dancing Fox: Arctic Folktales.*
    Illus. by Mary K. Okheena. New York: Morrow.
Bierhorst's straightforward retellings, extensive introduction to the Inuit, notes on the stories, and a list of references makes this collection of 18 traditional stories of the Inuit people in Alaska, Canada, and Greenland a valuable addition to folklore collections. (Folklore)

Brown, Don. (1997). *Alice Ramsey's Grand Adventure.* Boston: Houghton.
In this picture book, Brown tells how 22-year-old Alice Ramsey drove from New York City to San Francisco in a Maxwell touring car in 1909. In completing this 59 day adventure, Ramsey became the first woman to motor across the U.S. (Biography)

Brown, Margaret Wise. (1997) *Goodnight Moon.* Illus. by Clement Hurd. New York: HarperCollins.
A bunny's bedtime ritual involves saying goodnight, in a rhythmic pattern, to everything he sees from his bed. This new edition of Brown's classic picture book includes a 50th anniversary retrospective by Leonard S. Marcus. (Picture book)

Byars, Betsy. (1997). *Ant Plays Bear.* Illus. by Marc Simont. New York: Viking.
This companion to *My Brother Ant* (1996) contains four more amusing, easy-to-read stories about irrepressible Ant (Anthony) and his older brother. (Beginning reader)

Davies, Nicola. (1997). *Big Blue Whale.* Illus. by Nick Maland. Cambridge, MA: Candlewick.
An engaging text and carefully detailed pen and ink illustrations washed with soft colors provide basic information about the physical characteristics, behavior, and habitat of "the biggest creature that has ever lived on Earth!" (Nonfiction)

Duke, Kate. (1998). *One Guinea Pig is Not Enough.* New York: Dutton.
"One guinea pig is a lonely guinea pig" but, when nine more guinea pigs are added in, one by one, you have a lot of guinea pig fun—and a delightful simple addition book. (Picture book)

Egielski, Richard. (1997). *The Gingerbread Boy.* New York: HarperCollins.
Egielski's gingerbread boy runs through New York City, eluding a woman, a man, a rat, a crew of construction workers, a quartet of street musicians, and a park policeman on a horse before he is devoured by a fox in the city zoo. (Picture book)

Florian, Douglas. (1998). *Insectlopedia.* San Diego: Harcourt.
In this companion volume to *Beast Feast* (1994), *On the Wing* (1996), and *In the Swim* (1997), Florian offers short inventive poems about insects (mayfly, praying mantis, hornet, weevils...) and other arthropods. Florian's watercolor portraits of these invertebrates build on the playfully integrated realistic and anthropomorphic images created in the poems. (Poetry)

Gannett, Ruth Stiles. (1997). *Three Tales of My Father's Dragon.* Illus. by Ruth Chrisman Gannett. New York: Random.
To celebrate the 50th anniversary of *My Father's Dragon*, Random House has published this collection of all three of the fantastic adventures of Elmer Elevator and a baby flying dragon named Boris: *My Father's Dragon*, *Elmer and the Dragon*, and *the Dragons of Blueland.* (Fiction)

George, Kristine O'Connell. (1997). *The Great Frog Race and Other Poems.* Illus. by Kate Kiesler. New York: Clarion.
George's poems share a young girl's moments of wonder and joy at experiencing life in the country. Kiesler's stunning oil paintings capture the girl's everyday—yet very special and memorable—explorations. (Poetry)

Ginsburg, Mirra. (1997). *Clay Boy.* Illus. by Jos. A. Smith. New York: Greenwillow.
In this free adaptation of a traditional Russian folktale, an old man and his wife who long for a child fashion a clay boy. The clay boy comes to life and begins to eat everything in sight (including Grandpa and Grandma). What will stop this clay boy with an insatiable appetite? His attempt to devour a butting goat. (Folklore)

Greene, Rhonda Gowler. (1997). *Barnyard Song.* Illus. by Robert Bender. New York: Atheneum.
It all started with "the sneeze of Bee buzzing on the autumn breeze." An epidemic of the barnyard flu causes the animal choir to go off key— "Cock-a-SQUAWK!-le-doo." With some TLC from the farmer, however, the animals are soon once again singing their barnyard song from dawn to dusk. (Picture book)

Halpern, Shari. (1997). *Hush, Little Baby.* New York: North-South. Halpern uses collages made with different types of paper painted with acrylics and watercolors and color photocopies of pieces of fabric to create bordered story quilt illustrations for this favorite lullaby. Here, however, it is mama not papa who is soothing the baby. A simple musical arrangement is included. (Nursery rhymes & songs)

Hamilton, Virginia. (1997). *A Ring of Tricksters: Animal Tales From America, the West Indies, and Africa.* Illus. by Barry Moser. New York: Blue Sky/Scholastic.
Master storyteller Hamilton retells 11 tales of tricksters: Bruh Rabbit, Anansi, and other crafty critters. Hamilton considers the origins and migration of these trickster tales in her introduction and provides source notes. (Folklore)

In Daddy's Arms I am Tall: African Americans Celebrating Fathers (1998). Illus. by Javaka Steptoe. New York: Lee & Low.
Poems by African American poets and Steptoe's beautifully composed mixed media illustrations celebrate the special bonds between fathers and their children. Biographical notes on the poets and a note about the materials and techniques Steptoe used to create the illustrations are included. (Poetry)

Janeczko, Paul B. (1998). *That Sweet Diamond: Baseball Poems.* Illus. by Carole Katchen. New York: Atheneum.
Janeczko's poems—"The Pitcher," "Catcher Sings the Blues," "The Infield," "Vendors," "Things to Do During a Rain Delay," and 14 more—cover various aspects of baseball, on and off the field. Katchen captures the atmosphere of the ballpark in the illustrations, done in pastels, that accompany the poems. (Poetry)

Karas, G. Brian. (1998). *The Windy Day. New York:* Simon & Schuster.
One day a wind whooshes into a tidy little town and changes everything, including the "h-o-o-o-o-o-hummmmmmmm" life of a tidy little boy named Bernard. (Picture book)

Kennedy, Dorothy M. (Ed.) (1998). *Make Things Fly: Poems About the Wind.* Illus. by Sarah Meret. New York: McElderry.
Twenty-seven poems by writers such as John Ciardi, Christina Rossetti, and Eve Merriam create vivid images of the wind. Meret's pencil drawings reflect the many moods of the wind presented in the poems. (Poetry)

King, Dr. Martin Luther, Jr. (1997). *I Have a Dream.* New York: Scholastic.
Fifteen Coretta Scott King Award and Honor Book artists contribute paintings to illustrate the famous speech delivered by Dr. King on August 28, 1963, in Washington, D.C. There is an introduction by Coretta Scott King, biographical notes on Dr. King, and statements by each of the illustrators about their interpretative artwork. (Nonfiction)

Leavy, Una. (1997). *Irish Fairy Tales and Legends.* Illus. by Susan Field. Boulder, CO: Roberts Rinehart.
A collection of ten Irish tales, including "The Children of Lir," "Tír Na N-Óg" (a variant of the King Midas story), and Fionn MacCumhail stories. Source notes and a pronunciation guide are included. Field's richly colored illustrations complement the heroism, trickery, magic, romance, and humor of these well-told tales. (Folklore)

Lionni, Leo. (1997). *Frederick's Fables: A Treasury of 16 Favorite Leo Lionni Stories.* New York: Knopf.
Lionni's best-loved animal characters—Alexander, Swimmy, Cornelius, Frederick, and others—appear in this reissued collection of stories (originally published in 1985). (Picture storybook)

Livingston, Myra Cohn (Ed.). (1997). *I am Writing a Poem About...: A Game of Poetry.* New York: McElderry.
In her master class in poetry at UCLA, Livingston had students play a poetry game. The first assignment was to use one given word—rabbit— in a poem; the second was to use three given words—ring, drum, and blanket; and the final one was to use six words—hole, friend, candle, ocean, snake and bucket or scarecrow. The poems in this collection are some of the results of their playing with words. (Poetry)

Lobel, Arnold. (1997). *The Arnold Lobel Book of Mother Goose.* New
    York: Knopf.
Lobel's love for the old verses is evident in this large, cleverly illustrated
volume of more than 300 timeless nursery rhymes. A reissue of *The
Random House Book of Mother Goose* (1986). (Nursery rhymes &
songs)

Lowell, Susan. (1997). *Little Red Cowboy Hat.* Illus. by Randy Cecil.
    New York: Holt.
In this southwestern version of the traditional story of Little Red Riding
Hood, spunky Little Red and her self-reliant Grandma ("This time he
picked the wrong grandma.") rid the ranch of the pesty big gray wolf
forever. (Picture book)

Lullabies: An Illustrated Songbook. (1997). Musical arrangements by
    Richard Kapp. San Diego: Gulliver/Harcourt.
A collection of 37 well-loved nursery songs representing a variety of
musical styles and traditions, from anonymous folk songs to lullabies by
famous composers and poets. Each song is given a brief introduction
and paired with works of art from the Metropolitan Museum of Art.
(Nursery rhymes & songs)

MacDonald, Elizabeth. (1998). *The Wolf is Coming!* Illus. by Ken
    Brown. New York: Dutton.
"The Wolf is coming!" and the rabbits scurry to the chicken coop. Their
safety is brief, however, as the hen spies the approaching wolf. Rabbits
and chickens head for the pigsty. More and more animals gather, until a
rickety old shack overcrowded with animals seeking shelter from the
hungry wolf collapses and the explosion of animals—rabbits, chickens,
pigs, cows, and a donkey—onto the ground frightens the wolf away.
(Picture book)

Markle, Sandra and Markle, William. (1998). *Gone Forever!: An
    Alphabet of Extinct Animals.* Illus. by Felipe Dá valos. New York:
    Atheneum.
An alphabet of fascinating animals that are now gone forever, from the
auroch (a wild oxen) to Burchell's zebra. The Markles provide basic
information about the characteristics of the animals and factors relating
to their extinction. The inclusion of "animals that lived much more

recently than dinosaurs" but are now extinct helps young readers understand the need to protect endangered species today. (Nonfiction)

Miller, William. (1997). *Richard Wright and the Library Card.* Illus. by Gregory Christie. New York: Lee & Low.
A 17-year-old African American borrows a white man's library card so that he can check out books from the public library, a privilege denied him in the segregated South of the 1920s. Based on a scene from Wright's autobiography, *Black Boy.* (Picture book/biography)

Mochizuki, Ken. (1997). *Passage to Freedom: The Sugihara Story.* Illus. by Dom Lee. New York: Lee & Low.
In 1940, Chiune Sugihara, the Japanese consul to Lithuania, disobeyed his government's orders and issued thousands of visas to Jewish refugees so that they could escape the Nazis. *Passage to Freedom* is narrated by a five-year-old Hiroki, Chiune Sugihara's son. (Nonfiction)

Mora, Pat. (1997). *Tomás and the Library Lady.* Illus. by Paul Colón. New York: Knopf.
Tomás, a young migrant worker in Iowa, is befriended by a librarian and soon is reading borrowed books and telling stories to his family. This story has its roots in the real life story of Tomás Rivera, who became chancellor of the University of California at Riverside. (Picture book)

Opie, Iona (Ed.). (1996). *My Very First Mother Goose.* Illus. by Rosemary Wells. Cambridge, MA: Candlewick.
Folklorist Opie has selected more than 60 traditional rhymes and Wells has created joyous watercolor illustrations for this anthology that will charm children and adults alike. A set of four board books is also available: *Humpty Dumpty and Other Rhymes* (1997); *Little Boy Blue and Other Rhymes* (1997); *Pussycat Pussycat and Other Rhymes* (1997); and *Wee Willie Winkie and Other Rhymes* (1997). Each book features eight of the rhymes from *My Very First Mother Goose.* (Nursery rhymes & songs)

Osborne, Mary Pope. (1998). *Favorite Medieval Tales.* Illus. by Troy Howell. New York: Scholastic.
A collection of nine well-told, well-known tales from medieval Europe, including "Beowulf," "Sir Gawain and the Green Knight," "The Sword

in the Stone," and "The Song of Roland." An introduction, notes on the stories, artist's notes, bibliography, and index are included. (Folklore)

Peck, Jan. (1998). *The Giant Carrot*. Illus. by Barry Root. New York: Dial.
In this delightfully humorous tale, the giant turnip of the classic Russian folktale is a whopping big carrot and the Russian peasants are replaced by barefooted country folk: Papa Joe, Mama Bess, Brother Abel, and Little Isabelle. It is sweet Little Isabelle who is responsible for the carrot's tremendous growth and its harvest. Root extends the down-on-the-farm flavor of this outrageous story. A recipe for Little Isabelle's Carrot Puddin' is included. (Folklore)

Philip, Neil (Ed.). (1997). *Fairy Tales of the Brothers Grimm*. Illus. by Isabelle Brent. New York: Viking.
The storyteller's voice is strong in Philip's retellings of the 20 fairy tales in this anthology, which is illuminated by Brent's intricately designed full-page illustrations and framed with gold and blue borders. Philip's introduction outlines the publishing history of these tales by Jacob and Wilhelm Grimm. (Folklore)

Pinkney, Jerry. (1997). *Rikki-tikki-tavi*. New York: Morrow.
Pinkney has created a beautiful picture book edition of Rudyard Kipling's timeless tale from *The Jungle Book* about the feisty mongoose who engages in a life-and-death struggle with Nag and Nagarina, two deadly cobras. (Picture book)

Plourde, Lynn. (1997). *Pigs in the Mud in the Middle of the Rud*. Illus. by John Schoenherr. New York: Blue Sky/Scholastic.
It has rained and poured and now the family's Model T Ford is "stopped in the rud by some pigs in the mud." The pigs won't budge and, to make matters worse, they are soon joined by hens, sheep, and bulls. (Picture book)

Prelutsky, Jack (Ed.). (1997). *The Beauty of the Beast: Poems From the Animal Kingdom*. Illus. by Meilo So. New York: Knopf.
A collection of more than 200 poems about animals, organized into five sections: In Trillions We Thrive (insects and other invertebrates); Jubilant, We Swim (aquatic animals); Dragons in Miniature (Reptiles);

Hollow-Boned Singers (Birds); and Wrapped in Coats of Fur (mammals). Prelutsky has written a short poem to introduce each section. Indexed by title and author; bibliographical references. (Poetry)

Riley, Linnea. (1997). *Mouse Mess.* New York: Blue Sky/Scholastic. Riley uses a spare rhyming text and brightly colored cut paper illustrations to tell the story of a mouse who raids a tidy kitchen in search of a late night snack. In doing so, Mouse leaves a terrible mess, which he attributes to the homeowners ("Mouse steps back. He looks around./ He can't believe the mess he's found./ "Who made this awful mess?" asks Mouse./ "These people need to clean their house!"") (Picture book)

Roddie, Shen. (1998). *Too Close Friends.* Illus. by Sally Anne Lambert. New York: Dial.
Hippo and Pig are neighbors and fast friends. When Hippo cuts down the tall hedge between their houses, however, the loss of privacy threatens to destroy their friendship. (Picture book)

Rylant, Cynthia. (1998). *Henry and Mudge and the Sneaky Crackers.* Illus. by Suçie Stevenson. New York: Simon & Schuster.
This sixteenth adventure of Henry and his big dog, Mudge, in which Henry buys a spy kit complete with secret codes and spy glasses and the pair take up sleuthing (Mudge gets to wear a fedora), is just as much fun as the first book in this superb series for young independent readers. (Beginning readers)

Rylant, Cynthia. (1998). *Mr. Putter and Tabby Toot the Horn.* Illus. by Arthur Howard. San Diego, CA: Harcourt.
In this latest book about elderly Mr. Putter and his old yellow cat, Tabby, their neighbor Mrs. Teaberry decides that she and Mr. Putter should join a band. (Beginning readers)

Silverman, Erica. (1998). *On the Morn of Mayfest.* Illus. by Marla Frazee. New York: Simon & Schuster.
In this cumulative rhyme, a sleepwalking girl inadvertently starts a Pied Piper-like parade of people and animals (dove, huntsman, mouse, cat, sheep dog, laundress…) on the morn of Mayfest. Frazee's illustrations offer a beautifully detailed Medieval setting for this delightful spring frolic. (Picture book)

Simont, Marc. (1997). *The Goose That Almost Got Cooked.* New York: Scholastic.
Doing flips and loop-the-loops instead of staying in V-formation with the other migrating Canada Geese exhausts and grounds Emily. She takes up residence with seven domestic geese. Farm life seems perfect until the farmer's wife decides to have a wild goose dinner. (Picture book)

Stoeke, Janet Morgan. (1997). *A Friend for Minerva Louise.* New York: Dutton.
In her fourth adventure, this inquisitive hen's feather-brained perceptions lead her to conclude that all the changes she spies in the farm house ("a new wheelbarrow" (pram), " a new rabbit hutch" (crib), ...) must be due to the arrival of a new bunny in the family. (Picture book)

Taback, Simms. (1997). *There was an Old Lady Who Swallowed a Fly.* New York: Viking.
In Taback's illustrations for this popular nursery song, the old lady who swallowed a fly gets progressively larger as she swallows a series of animals—spider, bird, cat, dog, cow, and horse—in an absurd attempt to rectify the original mishap. Die-cut holes show the contents of the old lady's stomach. The illustrations are filled with interesting details and wacky asides. Caldecott Honor Book. (Folklore)

Vagin, Vladimir. (1998). *The Enormous Carrot.* New York: Scholastic.
In this adaptation of a traditional Russian folktale, the enormous turnip that won't come up is replaced by an enormous carrot and the peasants by rabbits Daisy and Floyd, who find the carrot growing amidst their hollyhocks and sunflowers. (Folklore)

Van Laan, Nancy. (1998). *The Magic Bean Tree: A Legend from Argentina.* Illus. by Beatriz Vidal. Boston: Houghton.
In this tale that explains why the shade of the carob tree is considered to bring luck, a young Quechuan boy sets out on his own to bring the rains back to his drought-stricken homeland. Vidal's folk art style illustrations offer beautiful scenes of the Argentine pampas. Glossary and source notes. (Folklore)

Van Laan, Nancy. (1998). *With a Whoop and a Holler: A Bushel of Lore From Way Down South.* New York: Atheneum.
The title and subtitle say it all. This is a delightful collection of short stories, rhymes, superstitions, and sayings from three regions of the South: the Bayou, the Deep South, and the Great Smokies and Blue Ridge Mountains. Van Laan's retellings and Cook's illustrations are fresh and funny. Source notes. (Folklore)

Wahl, Jan. (1998). *The Singing Geese.* Illus. by Sterling Brown. New York: Lodestar.
In this African American tall tale, Sam Bombel shoots a singing goose and his wife dresses and cooks it. But just as Sam is about to carve the roasted goose, a flock of geese fly in the window and gives Sam such an outrageous surprise that he never goes hunting again. (Folklore)

Waugh, Sylvia. (1997). *Mennyms Alive.* New York: Greenwillow.
In this fifth book about the Mennyms, the family of life-sized rag dolls with the ability to think, speak, and move come back to life (Sir Magnus' premonition that life would leave all of them at the same moment on October 1 proved true in *Mennyms Alone* (1996)) and search for a suitable residence where they can be safe from human eyes and live happily ever after. (Fiction)

Wells, Rosemary. (1997). *Bunny Cakes.* New York: Dial.
Bunny siblings Max and Ruby are making surprise birthday cakes for Grandma. Ruby's is an angel surprise cake decorated with raspberry-fluff icing and silver stars, sugar hearts, and buttercream roses; Max's is an earthworm cake iced with caterpillar frosting and topped off with Red-Hot Marshmallow Squirters. Grandma doesn't know which cake to dig into first. (Picture book)

Wells, Rosemary. (1997). *Bunny Money.* New York: Dial.
Ruby plans on buying Grandma a music box with skating ballerinas. Bunny money, however, has a way of slipping through fingers when Max is along on a shopping trip. The inexpensive presents that the pair finally do purchase—bluebird earrings that play "Oh, What a Beautiful Morning" and a set of glow-in-the-dark vampire teeth—thrill Grandma nonetheless. (Picture book)

Wells, Rosemary. (1998). *Max's Bath*; *Max's Bedtime*; *Max's Birthday*; *Max's Breakfast*; *Max's First Word*; *Max's New Suit*; *Max's Ride*; and *Max's Toys*. New York: Dial.
These eight toddler-pleasing stories in the Max Board Book series (originally published in 1985) have been reissued with new illustrations. (Board books)

Wells, Rosemary. (1997). *Noisy Nora*. New York: Dial.
Feeling neglected, middle child Nora engages in noisy and naughty activities to attract attention. Nothing works, however, until Nora gets too quiet. The larger format and full color art of this new edition (*Noisy Nora* was originally published in 1973) makes this a good choice for read-aloud sessions. (Picture book)

Zelinksy, Paul O. (1997). *Rapunzel*. New York: Dutton.
Zelinsky's exquisite oil paintings, with their beautifully detailed Italian Renaissance settings, make this version of the well-known fairy tale about a beautiful girl with long golden hair who is imprisoned in a tower by a sorceress a treasure. Caldecott Medal Book. (Folklore)

HAWAIIAN CHILDREN'S LITERATURE: GIVING A NEW VOICE TO AN ANCIENT CULTURE

Leilani Brown

Quiet warm rain sings
Of roots growing in lava
Flowers where flame was
Annette Schaefer Morrow, *Haiku of Hawaii*

Hawaiian children's literature today serves several important purposes; it is a window on the history and oral tradition of the Hawaiian people, it speaks eloquently of the grace and beauty of the culture and unique environment of the islands, and it is a vehicle for restoring the Hawaiian language to its rightful place in modern Hawaiian society. The history of Hawaii is filled with a rich oral tradition of songs, stories, chants, and poetry that guided, inspired, and enriched the lives of the early Polynesians who set out in open canoes, carrying all that was necessary to begin a new life. In their minds they carried their history, their gods, their poetry, their humor and folklore, and their dances. As they sailed, they sang, told stories, laughed, and taught their children to sing, to dance, and to remember by repetition. This oral tradition inspired the people, providing them with strength and confidence on the long voyage. The ocean and its creatures, the stars that lit the sky, and the birds that flew beside them all had a place in that important oral tradition. On this voyage, many beautiful places were discovered and settled. Hawaii was one of those beautiful places.

The islands of Polynesia fit into a neat triangle, with Hawaii at the north tip, New Zealand at the south, and Easter Island at the eastern tip. Set like jewels in the vast area of ocean within this triangle are the tiny volcanic islands known as the Ring of Fire. On all these islands, a rich oral tradition provided the basis for a number of distinct cultures with their own unique forms of dance, song, story, and poetry based on an intimate knowledge of nature and the physical/spiritual environment known as the *aina* in Hawaii.

Where did the original Polynesians come from? The poets sing of a lush green, much loved place, Hawaiki, after which Hawaii is named. It may have been India or coastal Southeast Asia, although history is unclear. Of all the migrations in human history, the Polynesian dispersal and settlement are unusual, resembling a flight of birds to beautiful places unknown. Perhaps it is because the Polynesians discovered and settled the last uninhabited land in the world, small islands of spectacular beauty and isolation, that their oral tradition has evolved into distinct cultures with a beauty and subject matter all their own.

A Brief History of the Oral Tradition of Hawaii

When the Polynesians arrived in Hawaii, they came upon a new land where life was warm and easy. In this land, material possessions were of less importance than the power of place. This new place had a powerful *aina* that included a volcano, rain forests, unique birds, animals, waterfalls, food, and flowers. The topics of songs and stories began to include these aspects of the environment interwoven with universal topics such as love, courtship, warfare, trickery, and the deeds of some powerful new deities.

One of the most important of these new deities was Pele, the beautiful and terrible goddess of Kilauea volcano. Legend says that Pele's spirit flew across the sea from Tahiti and took up residence in Halemaumau crater on Kilauea. Powerful, temperamental, and unpredictable, Pele became an important part of Hawaiian religion. In her was the power to create new land or to destroy forests and villages with the lava that flowed down the slopes of Kilauea. Stories of Pele and her deeds of terror, revenge, and kindness abound in the oral tradition of Hawaii. By understanding and believing in the goddess Pele, the Hawaiian people gained a deeper understanding of their new environment and learned how to live with the volcano and its unpredictable and awesome power.

Today, even though Christianity has long been present in Hawaii, Pele is still very much alive in the culture and tradition of Hawaii. Legends of Pele fill the pages of children's and adult's books. When walking on the volcano, it is common to see symbols of respect to Pele in the form of one or two lava rocks wrapped in green ti leaves stacked one upon the other. It is considered forbidden to remove lava rocks from Hawaii. The legend of "Pele's curse" says that anyone who takes lava from Hawaii will suffer bad luck, ill health, or even death, until the rocks are returned. Like many powerful legendary figures, Pele often changes her form and disguises herself as an old, white-haired woman. Many stories, some of them quite recent, tell of the experiences of children and adults who met an old woman while walking on the volcano or on a hiking trail in Volcanoes National Park. Good fortune or ill may follow those who encounter the old woman, depending on their behavior toward her or the volcano itself.

There are several types of lava present on the volcano slopes. Each of these types of lava has a name. The long black strands of spun glass that are seen caught in the cracks of the lava flow are known as Pele's hair. It is considered good fortune to find this kind of lava.

Pele is often the subject of Hawaiian art. She is painted regularly in her home in Halemaumau crater. In the drawing below, she is pictured sparing the village of the small girl in the lower left of the drawing (Puku'i, 1996).

The Hawaiian Language

The Hawaiian alphabet consists of only twelve characters. When speaking Hawaiian, each vowel is pronounced. Double vowels are common, such as in the word *alii* (ah lee ee) which means royalty, or *o'opu* (oh oh poo) which is the word for fish. There is a short poem designed to teach keikis (children) the alphabet. There is a second poem for teaching children to count. These Hawaiian nursery rhymes are used in many schools and are usually set to music.

The Hawaiian Alphabet

A is aloha (ah low ha) Aloha is love
E is 'ekahi (a kah hee) Ekahi is one
I is ipu (ee poo) Ipu is gourd
O is o'opu (oh oh poo) O'opu is a fish

He is hele (heh lay) Let's go out to play
Ke is keiki (kay kee) Keiki is a child I say
La is lani (lah nee) Lani is sky
Mu is mu'mu (moo moo) What a pretty dress I have
Nu is nuha (noo ha) I'm sad and blue
Pi is piko (pee koh) See my belly button, too
We is wela (vel ah) It's a hot sunny day
O Kina ' (oh kee nah) is the last letter we say

Count in Hawaiian

Ekahi (a kah hee) is one
Elua (a loo ah) is two
'A'ohe kama'a (ah oh hay kah ma ah) no more shoes
Ekolu (a koh loo) is three
Eha (a ha) is four
Pani i ka puka (pah nee ee kah poo kah) shut the door
Elima (a lee ma) is five
Eono (a oh no) is six
Honi ia'u (ho nee ee ah oo) Give me a kiss
Ehiku (a hee koo) is seven
Ewalu (a wah loo) is eight
Mai lulohi (my loo loh hee) Don't be late
Eiwa (a ee vah) is nine
Umi (oo me) is ten
Olelo hou (oh lay lo ho) Say it again

Children learn Hawaiian when they are preschoolers by hearing it spoken in the classroom and by looking at picture books that identify Hawaiian words. Bess Press has published an entire series of board books for this purpose, under the general heading of *Keiki's First Books*. The University of Hawaii Press has several books designed to introduce the beauty of the Hawaiian language, including Stephanie Feeney's *Hawaii is a Rainbow*, a book which teaches colors through an appreciation of the beauty of the islands.

The Punana Leo Hawaiian Language Immersion Program

'Aha Punana Leo, Inc. is a non-profit organization established in 1983 to serve the Hawaiian speaking community and focus on education through Hawaiian language. Punana Leo preschools, the first Native American language immersion program in the United States, began the process of revitalizing Hawaiian in 1984 through full day programs conducted entirely in Hawaiian. Hawaiian had by then become nearly extinct as a result of a government ban in 1896 forbidding instruction of children in Hawaiian language. Some of the concepts of the Punana Leo program are based on the Maori tradition (Schutz, 1995). The word Punana Leo translates *language nests*.

The Hawaiian language reappeared in public schools in 1987 when the first Punana Leo graduates entered elementary school. The program is now proceeding with plans to present Hawaiian language in middle and high school settings. 'Aha Punana Leo provides materials, curriculum, teacher training, family programs, and other services as well as the internationally known Punana Leo schools.

'Aha Punana Leo also publishes a variety of books that are Hawaiian language translations with Hawaiian songs and music on audiotape to accompany the books.

Translations of the books are also available in French and German as well as English. Two examples of books available from Aha Punana Leo are *'Ai'ai* by Kawika Napoleon; a story of the giant eel Ko'ona and the first fishpond built in Hawaii, and *'O Maile, Ka Pua'a* by Lilinoe Andrews; the adventure of Pilialoha and her parents as they were riding in a truck from Hilo to Waimea and found Maile the pig.

For more information, book lists, or materials lists, write or call:

Punana Leo Project   'Aha Punana Leo, Inc.
Hale Kako'o Punana Leo   1744 Kino'ole St.
2002 Hunnewell St.   Hilo, HI 96720
Honolulu, HI 96822
808-941-0584

The concepts, ideas, and teaching methods employed in the Punana Leo program may be successfully applied to other language learning or language immersion programs. The added pleasure of a multidimensional approach, integrating music and dance with reading and storytelling, is popular with students as well as teachers.

Significant Characters in Hawaiian Children's Literature

Some of the most significant and memorable characters in Hawaiian children's literature are animals, such as the delightful little gecko lizards. *The Legend of the Laughing Gecko* by Bruce Hale teaches a gentle lesson about acceptance, while *Goodnight Gecko* by Gill McBarnet shows a mother gecko dispelling her sons fears while teaching about the delightful sights of a Hawaiian night. Children's books are filled with gecko characters in Hawaii. Every house in Hawaii has its geckos, chirping in the night, catching insects, and stealing sips of juice from glasses left on the counter.

The mongoose is another creature of Hawaii that has found its way into the hearts of children's authors and young readers. Originally introduced to Hawaii to control the rat population and to protect against snake invasions, the mongoose has thrived and can be seen on most islands, inhabiting the tall grasses of the roadside and field. Alas, the mongoose is a day hunter and rats are nocturnal, but one can still run through snakeless grass barefoot thanks to the crafty and comical little mongoose. *Moki Mongoose Finds a Friend* by Deborah C. Taylor is the story of a lonely little mongoose that, searching for a friend who is just like himself, tries to befriend a coconut and learns that friends come in all shapes and sizes. From 'Aha Punana Leo comes *Ko Sepa Paikikala*, the story of Sepa the mongoose, his bicycle, and his many, assorted friends.

Pigs play a major role in Hawaiian children's literature just as they seem to do in British and American children's literature. The ancient Polynesians carried pigs with them in their canoes and so introduced them to the islands, where they are not always welcome in certain delicate environments. In children's literature, however, they are quite welcome, as in young children's books such as *Aunty Pua's Dilemma,* by

Ann Kondo Corum, the story of a pig with a very big problem, who learns to be happy with who she is. And the lovable Maile, the pig who is found by a little girl and her family as they are driving to Waimea from Hilo on the Big Island in 'Aha Punana Leo's *'O Maile, Ka Pua'a* by Lilinoe Andrews. In *Curious Kimo*, by Malia Maness, Kimo the pig is instructed not to cross over a stone wall. When he disobeys in his search for a guava fruit, he learns an important lesson.

Ireland has its leprechauns, England has its fairies, and Hawaii has menehunes (men ee hoo nees), the little people who do good deeds and are somewhat mischievous. The little menehunes especially enjoy children and animals, and they often get themselves into more than a little trouble. In *The Menehune and the Nene*, by Susan Yamashita, there are four menehune and one nene (nay nay) goose egg. By the time the four menehune decide what to do with the egg, it hatches. The baby goose repays them for their care by saving them from an erupting volcano. Menehunes add to the magical quality of the Hawaiian aina. In *Friends of the Menehune* by Karen Lei Noland, a little boy and his sister go for a hike in search of the menehune. When they find them, they become fast friends.

The Hawaiian deities are found often in children's literature and one in particular has a special appeal. Maui the demi-god is found at every level of children's literature. It is Maui who is credited with pulling the Hawaiian Islands up from the bottom of the sea with his magical fishhook in the young children's book, *Maui Goes Fishing* by Julie Stewart-Williams. In another picture storybook, *How Maui Slowed the Sun*, by Suelyn Ching Tune, Maui slows the sun and makes the day longer by pulling on the sun's legs with his magic lasso. In this way, the Hawaiian people were able to grow food. In another book by the same author, Maui humorously forces the mud hens to tell him the secret of how to make fire (*Maui and the Secret of Fire*). The young adult book, *Maui the Demigod*, by Steven Goldsberry, is a superb weaving of the tale of Maui's life and many adventures.

Pele, the goddess of the volcano, is a powerful force about whom many legends and myths abound. Herb Kawainui Kane has written a superb collection of myths, romances, folktales, and legends of the spectacular goddess in the young adult book, *Pele.* It is enhanced by the author's talented illustrations.

Honu the green sea turtle is famous in children's literature for being the first turtle to have a shell in *How Honu the Turtle Got His Shell* by Casey A. McGuire-Turcotte. Honu means turtle in the Hawaiian language, so most turtle characters are named Honu (ho noo). The non-fiction picture book, *Honu,* by Marion Coste, explains the life cycle of the green sea turtle while also explaining its endangered status.

Humpback whales visit Hawaii's warm waters each winter, staying to play and give birth in the warm waters from December until May. The whales are a very important part of Hawaiian culture, as are turtles and sharks (yes, sharks!) and in modern times the coming of the whales marks the coming of tourists to see the whales, the production of art featuring whales, dolphins, and the beautiful reef fishes, and all manner of celebrations of whales. *The Wonderful Journey* by Gil McBarnett allows readers to follow Kanani the whale and her mother as they make their annual migration northwards to the cold polar waters where they find food and new friends.

Sharks are greatly respected in the Hawaiian culture. The word and the name of the shark is Mano. In Hawaii, it is considered a great sin to kill a shark and the hunting of sharks is severely discouraged. Shark attacks are fairly rare in Hawaii and the large tiger shark is given respect and a wide berth in the ocean. The middle school book, *Red Shark,* by Ruth M. Tabrah is the story of a ninth grade boy who learns to come to respectful terms with the spirit of the island of Hawaii.

Finally, the Hawaiian people themselves are often central characters in the legends and stories that describe the many distinct periods of Hawaiian history from the time of King Kamehameha I to modern times. *Guns of Eden* by Ed Sheehan, is a young adult novel set in the 1700s, which describes the life of King Kamehameha I and John Young, as the king unites the islands. Interpersonal conflict is resolved when a part Hawaiian youth searches for identity in the myth-filled islands of Hawaii in John Dominis Holt's *Waimea Summer.*

The experiences of Japanese Americans on the sugar plantations of old Hawaii are chronicled in Milton Muryama's young adult book, *All I Asking for Is My Body*. One of the best adventure stories for grades 4, 5, and 6 is *Kalia and the King's Horse* by Gretel Blickhahn McLane. This book has a sensitive and deep understanding of the Hawaiian culture.

These books and many more like them are a source of understanding for all who wish to learn more about Hawaii and its rapidly changing present day culture and to learn something of its colorful history. Hawaiian children's literature provides a glimpse of the forces and events that have shaped Hawaii's culture in the past, a sample of the characters that play a part in its present day society, and an appreciation of the beauty and rhythm of a language that was almost lost.

References

Morrow, A. S. (1970). *Haiku of Hawaii*. Rutland, VT: Charles E. Tuttle Company.

Puku' i, M. K. (1996). *Hawai'i Island Legends*. Honolulu, HI: Kamehameha Schools Press.

Sinclair, M. (1982). *The Path of the Ocean*. Honolulu, HI: University of Hawaii Press.

Schutz, A. (1995). *All About Hawaiian*. Honolulu, HI: University of Hawaii Press.

Thompson, V. L. (1969). *Hawaiian Legends of Tricksters and Riddlers*. NY: Holiday House.

READING TO SURVIVE: EXPLORING THE COPING STRATEGIES OF AFRICAN AMERICANS

Gail L. Thompson

Abstract

This study examined the problems that two groups of African-American adults experienced during childhood and the coping strategies that they used. Data were gathered through interviews and a questionnaire. The findings indicate that racism, having had an unemployed parent, and the effects of parental divorce were the three most common problems that study participants experienced during childhood. Most of the participants relied upon socially acceptable strategies, such as prayer and hard work, to cope with problems. Moreover, three activities that are associated with school, reading, writing, and studying hard, were also important strategies that they used. These findings reveal that parents, ministers, and teachers can play important roles in helping children find non-destructive ways of coping with problems.

Introduction

Recent media reports have indicated that violence is becoming all too common among American youth. This violence was once seen as only a problem in inner cities and urban areas. Jones and Newman (1997), Kotlowitz (1991), and Shakur (1993) described communities in Chicago and Los Angeles that resemble war zones. Garbarino, et al. (1992) found that as a result of the chronic violence to which they are exposed, a substantial number of children in the U.S. suffer from the effects of Post Traumatic Stress Disorder. These symptoms include "re-experiencing the event, numbing of responsiveness, and symptoms of increased arousal" (Garbarino, et al. 1992, p. 75) and are common in individuals who have lived in war-torn countries in the Middle East and Southeast Asia. Today, however, violence among youth in America has spread beyond the inner cities and urban areas and occurs frequently in rural areas and small towns. Because the incidence of violence among youth is not only increasing in the U.S. but also affecting more children, strategies that enable children to cope with stress are invaluable. The current study examined the problems that African-American adults experienced during childhood and the ways in which they coped with these problems.

Method

Two methodologies, a questionnaire and interviews, were used. The quantitative data were based on 96 questionnaires that were returned from two Historically Black Colleges or Universities (HBCUs). To increase reliability, the questionnaire was field tested and used in a pilot study beforehand. Table 1 indicates the sections of the questionnaire that applied directly to the research questions.

All of the respondents were college juniors, seniors, or graduate students (see Table 2) who ranged in age from 19 to 51 years old. Males comprised 56 percent of the sample. The students grew up in 23 states. The majority was single. More than half were business majors and 28 percent were science majors. Fifty-nine percent of the students had a grade point average of 3.0 or higher.

In addition to the questionnaire data, narratives were also used to answer the research questions. These narratives were based on loosely structured interviews with 12 African-Americans, six males and six females, who were considered to be successful by traditional standards. They overcame various adversities that they experienced during childhood and/or adolescence and are now law-abiding citizens who are employed in professions that are associated with the middle and upper classes. Unlike the questionnaire, which permitted respondents to share their answers in an anonymous and impersonal manner, the interviews permitted respondents to share their answers face-to-face with the researcher or by telephone. Two of the key interview questions were similar to those that were used on the questionnaire (See Table 1).

Table 1

Key Interview Questions

Check any of the following problems or obstacles that you experienced when you were growing up and the *degree* to which the problem(s) *affected* you. Also write your *age* at the time when the event occurred.

	AGE	STRONGLY	MODERATELY	NOT AFFECTED
death of a parent(s)	—	—	—	—
divorce	—	—	—	—
an unemployed parent	—	—	—	—
alcoholic or drug using parent	—	—	—	—
physical abuse	—	—	—	—
incarcerated parent	—	—	—	—
racism or discrimination	—	—	—	—
homelessness	—	—	—	—
poverty	—	—	—	—
the death of a sibling	—	—	—	—
verbal abuse	—	—	—	—
a physical handicap	—	—	—	—
a learning disability	—	—	—	—
other_____	—	—	—	—

Check all of the strategies you used to deal with the aforementioned problems.

___ relying on a role model
___ prayer
___ reading
___ writing
___ studying hard
___ dreaming of a better life

___ hard work
___ avoiding the problem
___ substance abuse
___ retaliation
___ confrontation
___ other _____

With the exception of two biracial (half-White and half-Black) male
interviewees, who classified themselves as "Black" or "African
American," all of the interviewees were African-American adults. Most
of them were the only college graduates or one of the first college
graduates in the families in which they were reared. Two interviewees
had at least one parent who had been unable to attend school beyond
third grade. All of the interviewees except for one, who currently resides
in Washington, DC, were California residents at the time of the
interviews. Four were native Californians. The youngest interviewee
was 30 years old and the oldest (several) were in their early 50s.
Multiple regression was used to interpret the questionnaire data.
Intertextual analysis was used for the interviews.

Table 2
Student Status of Questionnaire Respondents

Status	Frequency	Percentage
Junior	35	37.2
Senior	41	43.6
Graduate	18	19.1
No Answer	2	Missing
Total	96	100.0

Results

Obstacles That the Interviewees
Experienced During Childhood

Many of the interviewees experienced several types of adversity
during childhood or adolescence, but in most cases one major obstacle
was predominant. One male interviewee lost his hearing during
adolescence. Several experienced poverty. Three were bullied by peers
or siblings. One was abused by her stepfather. Another had an alcoholic
mother and grandfather; he lived with this grandfather for the first 12
years of his life. One female interviewee experienced continuous racism
and hostility when she integrated an all-White high school. Another
interviewee was a sickly child. A male interviewee experienced the loss
of both parents during childhood. One male interviewee suffered the
effects of his parents' divorce during adolescence. A female interviewee

cited her rocky relationship with her father as the greatest problem that she experienced during childhood.

Obstacles That the College Students
Experienced During Childhood

The quantitative section of this study was based on the results of 96 questionnaires from African-American juniors, seniors, and graduate students. Nearly 30 percent of the students said that they did not experience any major problems during childhood or adolescence or they left this section of the questionnaire blank. Other students experienced one or more problems (see Table 3). Most students identified a certain age when the problem(s) began, but several said that they experienced problems continuously during childhood. For most of the problems that the students experienced, older children were more likely to be affected strongly, instead of moderately or not at all.

Table 3
Major Problems That the Respondents
Experienced During Childhood or Adolescence

Problem	Frequency	Percentage
racism/discrimination	28	29.2
unemployed parent	22	23.0
divorce	19	19.8
alcohol/drug-using parent	17	17.7
verbal abuse	15	15.6
death of a parent	13	13.5
poverty	8	8.3
death of a sibling	7	7.3
other problem(s)	6	6.3
learning disability	5	5.2
physical handicap	5	5.2
incarcerated parent	4	4.2
physical abuse	3	3.3
homelessness	2	2.3
Total	154	160.9

Racism/discrimination was the most frequently cited problem that the students experienced during childhood or adolescence, and it had a moderate or strong effect on 94 percent of those who experienced it. The average student was 13 years old at the time when the incident(s) occurred. Having an unemployed parent was the second most often cited problem, and it had a moderate or strong effect on 86 percent of the students in this category. The average student was 14 years old when his/her parent became unemployed. Divorce, the third most commonly cited problem, had a strong effect on 37 percent of the students who experienced this problem and a moderate effect on another 37 percent. The average student in this group was 10 years old when the divorce took place.

Having had a substance-abusing parent was the fourth most frequently cited problem. It had a strong effect on 59 percent of the students who experienced this problem and a moderate effect on 39 percent. The average student in this category was 10 years old when his/her parent became a substance abuser or when the student became aware of the problem. Verbal abuse had a strong or moderate effect on all of the respondents who experienced this problem. The average student who checked this problem was 10 years old when the verbal abuse began or when he/she became aware that it was a problem. The death of a parent, the sixth most frequently cited problem, had a strong effect on 85 percent of the students who lost a parent during childhood. The average student was 13 years old at the time. Homelessness, physical abuse, having had an incarcerated parent, a physical handicap, or a learning disability were the least cited problems.

Coping Strategies

The twelve interviewees used a variety of strategies to cope with the aforementioned problems. Three tried to avoid further conflicts by staying away from the individuals whom they perceived as antagonists. Two female interviewees found solace in books. At least two used optimism or a positive mindset to cope with problems. Two relied on the support of family members. One tried to become totally self-reliant. Another interviewee became more responsible at home and adopted the role of pseudo-father to his younger brother in order to cope with his parents' divorce. One interviewee mentioned that, in addition to other strategies, he used prayer to cope with his mother's death. Several interviewees--all women--mentioned that they used writing as a coping tool. The interviewee who integrated the all-White high school tried to rise above the hostile and dangerous situations in which she found herself. She also refused to take the hate mail and verbal and physical attacks personally. One interviewee took her hatred of her abusive stepfather out on a younger sister who was her stepfather's biological child. Another interviewee's dream of a better life helped her to cope with poverty.

During childhood and adolescence, the college students relied on numerous coping strategies (see Table 4) and certain problems were associated with certain strategies. Students who were strongly affected by racism/discrimination, divorce, parental unemployment, or a parent's substance abuse were likely to say that they had been very successful in overcoming the problems that they experienced during childhood. Those who had an unemployed parent, however, were most likely to say they had successfully overcome the effects of this problem.

Prayer, the most frequently cited coping strategy, was likely to be used by students who had a sibling die during childhood or adolescence but most likely to be used by students who had a learning disability. Hard work, the second most popular coping strategy, was most likely to be used by victims of racism/discrimination or physical abuse. Students who experienced poverty or a learning disability were likely to cope by dreaming of a better life. Victims of verbal abuse usually relied on studying hard to cope.

Role models appeared to be most beneficial in helping students cope with racism/discrimination or poverty. Nearly 88 percent of the respondents said that they had positive role models when they were growing up. Parents were the most popular role models, followed by other relatives, teachers and ministers, respectively. Famous person was the least cited role model, but nine percent of the students had famous role models.

Table 4
Coping Strategies That Respondents
Used During Childhood or Adolescence

Strategy	Frequency	Percentage
prayer	47	48.9
hard work	43	44.8
dreaming of a better life	26	27.1
studying hard	25	26.0
relying on a role model	24	25.0
reading	20	20.8
other strategies	18	18.7
avoiding the problem	17	17.7
confrontation	16	16.7
writing	15	15.6
retaliation	11	10.4
substance abuse	5	5.2
Total	267	276.9 N= 96

Nearly 21 percent of the students relied on reading as a way of dealing with problems. Those who were poor, had an incarcerated parent, or experienced racism/discrimination, the effects of parental divorce, or physical abuse were most likely to utilize this strategy. Victims of racism/discrimination and those who had parents who were substance abusers were likely to use writing as a coping strategy. Of the nearly 19 percent of the students who said that they had also relied on additional strategies that were not on the questionnaire, those who had a physical handicap were most likely to do so. Avoidance was utilized by students whose parents were substance abusers, some students whose parents divorced, and students who experienced racism/discrimination. Students who had an incarcerated parent, other problems that were not listed on the questionnaire, or who experienced verbal abuse, were likely to use confrontation to deal with these problems. Retaliation and substance abuse were the least cited coping strategies. Ten percent of the students said that they used retaliation. Students who were physically abused, had a learning disability, or other problems that were not listed on the questionnaire, were likely to use retaliation as a coping strategy. Five percent of the students said that they had relied on substance abuse as a coping strategy. Those who experienced poverty or who had an incarcerated parent were most likely to use this strategy.

Discussion

This study examined the ways in which two groups of African-American adults coped with problems that they experienced during childhood and/or adolescence. One group shared their stories through interviews. The other group, 96 students at HBCUs, completed a questionnaire.

Most of the participants experienced various problems during childhood, but 30 percent of the college students did not identify any major problem that they experienced. Racism/discrimination was the most frequently cited problem, having had an unemployed parent was second, and divorce was third. Homelessness, physical abuse, having had an incarcerated parent, a physical handicap, or a learning disability were the least cited problems.

The participants relied on a number of strategies to cope with their problems. Prayer, hard work, and dreaming of a better life were the most popular coping strategies. Retaliation and substance abuse were the least popular. Nearly 88 percent of the students said that they had positive role models during childhood, and 25 percent said that they relied on their role models as a way of coping with problems. Parents, other family members, and teachers, respectively, were the three most popular groups of role models. Individuals who had experienced racism and/or poverty were likely to use role models to cope with these problems.

Three categories of coping strategies that participants used were associated with school and/or literacy. Twenty-six percent of the participants said that they had coped with problems by studying hard. Victims of verbal abuse tended to be more likely to use this strategy. Nearly 21 percent of the participants said that they relied upon reading as a coping strategy during childhood. Those who had experienced racism, poverty, physical abuse, the effects of parental divorce, or had an incarcerated parent, were most likely to use this strategy. Nearly 16 percent of the students used writing as a coping strategy. Those who experienced racism or had a substance-abusing parent were most likely to use this strategy.

This study has several important implications. The first pertains to role models. Because the media tend to portray the African-American family as pathological, the fact that parents were the most popular group of role models and other family members was the second most popular group, is noteworthy. The message that some African-American parents are doing an exemplary job has not received enough attention by researchers or the media.

Second, because prayer was the most-commonly cited coping strategy, the implication that spirituality is important to African-Americans is apparent. The question, however, of "Which religious organizations are most effective in reaching African-American children?" deserves further study.

Finally, since teachers were the third most popular group of role models, this finding is also noteworthy. Obviously, many teachers are doing an outstanding job regarding their African-American students. Moreover, because a number of the participants relied on reading, writing, and studying hard as coping strategies, this finding deserves further research. The questions of "What made certain individuals resort to these coping strategies?" and "What methods were used to teach them to value these strategies?" warrant further exploration.

This study clearly shows that literacy is extremely valuable to African Americans. Aside from the obvious value of its being the foundation of academic success, its value as a way of coping with stress and problems was revealed. Today, Americans in all communities are in need of solutions to stem the tide of violence among youth. If more parents, teachers, and role models could convey the message that these activities (reading, writing, and studying hard) which tend to be associated with school, can also have cathartic value, perhaps fewer children and adolescents will feel the need to resort to violence to solve problems.

References

Garbarino, J., Dubrow, N., Kostelny, K., and Pardo, C. (1992). *Children in Danger: Coping with the Consequences of Community Violence.* San Francisco, CA: Jossey-Bass Publishers.

Jones, L., Newman, L., and Isay, D. (1997). *Our America: Life and Death on the South Side of Chicago.* NY: Scribner.

Kotlowitz, A. (1991). *There Are No Children Here.* NY: Anchor Books.

Shakur, S. (1993). *Monster: The Autobiography of an L.A. Gang Member.* NY: Penguin Books.

PHONICS IN CONTEXT WITHIN A MULTILINGUAL SETTING

Alejandro E. Jauregui

What is it about phonics instruction in the primary classrooms that makes teachers uneasy? Routman (1991) states that " the whole concept of phonics continues to be an emotional and political issue, and it does not seem likely that educators will ever come to a consensus" (p. 147). Most teachers feel strongly about how they teach phonics in their classrooms, yet feel self-conscious about telling others how they instruct their students. "Very few primary teachers actually talk about how they teach phonics, and most of them do it behind closed doors" (Routman, 1991, p. 147).

The dilemma we are facing as educators when it comes to phonics is not whether we should *teach* phonics, but rather *how* phonics should be taught meaningfully in the classroom. Knowing various teachers instruct their students using the "Whole Language" approach, or that others use numerous traditional methods, we as educators need to produce a set of universal goals and teaching methods that will help all students learn phonics effectively.

The purpose of this paper is to attempt to gain insight into the most thorough and effective techniques which will enable all students, including second language learners, with the knowledge and understanding of phonics in order to become successful readers and writers. Smith (1996) asks the question, "Is it possible for both phonics and reading and writing to occur simultaneously?" (p. 13). This paper will seek to answer questions of why, how, and when phonics should be taught. Through the focus of recent findings, educators and researchers will verify the answers to these questions. They will also shed light on the way phonics must be taught in order to provide the "essential" literacy needed for children of various language backgrounds growing up in the nineties and entering the twenty-first century.

The Role of Phonics Instruction and Literacy
in Teaching Second Language Learners

Phonics is not only important to students whose primary language instruction is in English, but also to students who speak another language in the home. In order to teach students learning English as a second language phonics, reading, and writing, we need to make sure that they have a firm cognitive foundation in their primary language. If not, they will experience difficulty in transferring their limited skills in their primary language to their second language instruction (Hamers & Blanc, 1989). Once students have gained proficiency in their first language, they will have the advantage of using both languages for academic as well as communicative tasks. This will transfer over into phonics instruction taught through the second language and will give students confidence to progress in the areas of reading and writing.

Students who have a firm grasp of reading and writing forms in their first language will be able to transfer these concepts to the second language to make sense of what the teacher wants them to grasp. Cummins (Hamers & Blanc, 1989) calls this the "Common Underlying Proficiency (CUP)" which states that both languages are working together to make sense of each other.

Krashen (1988) believes that second language learners need to be given comprehensible input during phonics as well as literature instruction. This means the teacher must give the second language student words already learned in the first language translated to the second language (English).

In addition, the teacher must provide some vocabulary not yet learned in the second language so that processing will occur mentally and the student will be challenged.

Lastly, in order to develop a firm cognitive grasp in phonics, reading, and writing within a second language learning student, Krashen (1988) believes students need to experience a low affective filter. In other words, students who feel taking academic risk will subject them to teacher criticism will avoid challenge. Therefore, an environment must be created for students that will build their self-concept and motivate them to take risks that will lead to success. Educators must create an environment in which affective filters can be facilitated. This can be done while organizing lessons, speaking, and responding to students so they can produce more positive gains cognitively in their second language.

All students, regardless of language background, need to develop a strong awareness of phonics within a balanced approach to reading. This means ensuring instruction in phonics is taught within meaningful reading and writing contexts. In addition, it is imperative that the educator comprehends reading instruction as a whole, without placing undue emphasis on any one element.

Why Phonics Should Be Taught

In order to fully understand the necessity of phonics instruction, we need to understand how students read words, and how they gain the relationship of attaching meaning to words by connecting sounds to letters, then letters to words. Routman (1991) states:

> Successful readers view reading as an interactive, meaning-getting process, and grapho-phonics is one of the necessary cueing systems they utilize. Proficient readers function with an interdependence between three cueing systems: semantics, syntax, and grapho-phonics. Semantic cues (context: what makes sense) and syntactic clues (structure and grammar: what sounds right grammatically) are strategies the reader needs to be using already in order for phonics (letter- sound relationships: what looks right visually and sounds right phonetically) to make sense (p. 147).

Students need to use the three basic cueing systems of semantics, syntax, and grapho-phonics together in order to make the reading process successful. Most often in the classroom, too much emphasis is put on the grapho-phonic system at any given time. This alone cannot elicit comprehension of text.

As educators we need to remember the importance of phonics as one part of the reading process, and its crucial balance with semantics and syntax. May (1990) states that good readers use grapho-phonics to decode new words by means of recognizing spelling patterns in known words. Stating that this system is merely having students "sound out" the words is not enough. Students need to be able to understand words and their meanings in order to develop the grapho-phonic as well as the syntactic and semantic cues in reading (p. 219).

Smith (1996, p. 13) also implies that reading is a process of *constructing meaning* from written texts. Students need to use their background knowledge and words from what they are reading, whether this is in their first or second language, in order to create meaning. If students have difficulty recognizing words, there will be an incomplete foundation for constructing meaning. Phonics should be used along with context, word parts, syntax, and automatically so that readers are able to recognize words. May (1990, p. 219) feels strongly that reading must not be a single cueing system, therefore phonics should not be taught in isolation. Reading needs to be thought of as an interactive process, one that involves students using all of their senses, learning styles, and comprehension techniques in order to comprehend text. In certain cases, it may be crucial to allow second language students to experience both languages simultaneously as another part of the learning process.

Most young children will have no clue as to how the sounds they are connecting with letters relate to reading (Routman, 1991, p. 148). This can be one problem that may occur when teaching phonics in isolation. If a child struggles with the reading progress, having to rely on the grapho-phonic cues as opposed to the semantic or syntactic can become very cumbersome. Children who have difficulty reading usually have learned to rely heavily on the least of the cueing systems, which is grapho-phonics. Instead of relying more on phonics, time must be spent on a balance of both phonics and reading of authentic texts.

All in all, phonics should be taught, since it is one of the three essential components of the cueing systems. However, in order to make phonics instruction successful, it must be done within a meaningful context for the learner. Students should not have to recite words or sounds that have no value to them or will not easily transfer mentally while reading authentic texts. Phonics is a necessary element for a child to become a successful reader. We must remember it is not an effective tool when used alone.

How Should Phonics Be Taught?

Knowing that phonics, semantics, and syntax work together to create a complete picture of the reading process, students should be taught in such a way that all cueing systems are taken into account. Morrow and Tracey (1997) feel that phonics should be taught in the context of reading and writing activities and should not be isolated. They strongly believe materials such as worksheets and flashcards are inappropriate. Instead, teachers should teach phonics skills naturally from activities in which the class is engaged (p. 645). Routman (1991) supports this standpoint as well. "Giving young children worksheets for flash letters and words in isolation is asking them to go from letter to sound—an unnatural and complicated task where some children have no success" (p. 148). Children naturally go from sound to letter when writing and using invented spelling. This proves to the educator that learning proceeds from the known to the unknown. When children start with real words which hold meaning for them, they can better hold the sound and connect it to a letter in their minds. The sound, regardless of which language the child uses, is useful then only in the context of a word that is already embedded in a meaningful sentence.

Phonics must develop from meaningful language experiences. May (1990) explains that in practice, teachers need to spend time developing oral language experiences (listening and speaking skills). This will then lead to writing and thus to meaningful use of grapho-phonic skills (p. 222). As teachers, we need to look to the child and carefully observe daily reading and writing behaviors so that we can know *how* to teach them phonics combining all of the cueing systems.

Smith (1996) feels there are three ways in which phonics should be taught. First, teaching children phonics within the context of reading and writing is vital in allowing them to see and hear phonics in action. Routman (1991) believes that it is perfectly acceptable to call attention to sounds and words students will need while reading and writing aloud in a small group or with the entire class. By using materials such as "Big Books" to read with children, we as educators are sensitive to the phonics and rhyming words that can be used practically within the context of specific literature. Rather than telling students what specific sounds and letters are, students must discover which sounds and rules works best for them. This will enable them to gain meaningful phonetic associations on their own (p.149).

Secondly, "Phonics instruction should be demonstrated as one of multiple cueing systems that are used in conjunction with one another" (Smith, 1996, p. 14). Children will use the grapho-phonic cueing system along with context and syntax of the text, the illustrations in the book, and the words they recognize automatically. The use of these multiple cueing systems allows children to achieve successful approximations. The English language is not completely phonetic, therefore, children will not be able to pronounce words or their spellings accurately simply by knowing phonics. When children are shown how to adjust and are praised for adjusting their initial attempts at spelling and reading, they are able to use their grapho-phonic knowledge flexibly.

Third, "Phonetic instruction should be aimed at developing automaticity" (Smith, 1996, p. 14). To become a fluent reader, it is important for students to identify words quickly so that they devote their energy and attention to comprehension rather than concentrating on each word or letters in that word. The focus at times needs to be on whole words as opposed to only sounds and letters in isolation. The more learners, particularly second language students, are exposed to print and words which are most frequently used in the English language, the more they can develop fluency as readers and writers. Children are then able to see a word, recall it, then move on to the next word in that sentence with ease.

Opportunities for ongoing phonics teaching and evaluation in the classroom come up daily in the following contexts. These techniques can be used to develop the three points stated by Smith in integrating phonetic instruction:

Students may read poems with the entire class highlighting sounds on a poem chart, then reading and re-reading for clarity. Students may also go through a technique with a teacher in a small group called "shared reading" where they predict, discuss, analyze, and read a certain book chorally. Radencich (1996) also explains that children need options in activities whenever possible (p. 31). Students can pair up and work well reading stories around the room, or writing around the room using a clipboard. Other students might enjoy making letters on the chalkboard with a wet paintbrush, while yet others might find success working with a phonics computer program. As long as phonics is taught within the context of reading and writing, it will be effective and will become meaningful to students.

Routman (1991) explains, "In meaningful phonics teaching, connections of sounds and letters are always made in real life contexts. Beyond the book or story, we lead children to make connections in other contexts—whether they be signs, labels, charts, calendars, poems, and even children's names" (p. 149). Students must be immersed in print everywhere they go, so they can connect sounds, letters, and words in every day situations. If letters become meaningful and useful to them, words will follow, and then sentence comprehension will ensue.

When is Instruction in Phonics the Most Productive?

Smith (1996) states that phonics instruction is most successful when students have a context in which to learn the phonetic code system (p. 15). Children who have experienced hours of exposure to print during their preschool years at home or at school enter kindergarten with a strong foundation for learning to read. If children are lacking this foundation, schools provide activities such as listening to stories, shared reading of big books, matching print to nursery rhymes, chants, and other language experience activities to promote phonetic awareness and instruction.

Students must be taught phonics whenever there is an opportunity to read and enjoy meaningful text. Routman (1991) feels there are plenty of opportunities within the school day to integrate phonics instruction into all subjects, as long as it is taught strategically in the meaning of context in predictable stories children read and write daily. Most of reading should be spent on reading for meaning, and most of writing is spent writing on self-selected topics, so children develop awareness of phonics naturally as they try to make sense of texts (p.149). Routman also realizes that not all children "pick up" phonics. She makes sure to discover and apply phonics generalizations by using literature and the children's need to determine the phonics necessary for those who need a systematic way of learning sound and letter relationships.

There is no "specified" time when children should officially begin to use phonics instruction. Powell and Hornsby (1993) explain, "It is apparent that the better the match between the reader's background knowledge and context (semantic and syntactic cues) the less attention the reader needs to give to grapho-phonic cues. Proficient readers will use grapho-phonic knowledge to confirm or reject their predictions. The grapho-phonic cues at the beginning of words, for example, are generally the most helpful" (p. 19). Children who are immersed in meaningful interactions between written text will be able to comprehend phonics within the whole context of reading.

Avery (1993) observed her own students during the writing process. She states that children do need to learn phonics within extremely meaningful contexts and at their own developmental levels.

> I watched my children write. I heard my students repeat a
> particular word over and over to themselves, listening for letters
> and perhaps searching for a visual recall of that word in order to
> write it for themselves. They didn't really sound out but they
> did seem to connect the names of letters to the sounds they heard
> when repeating words over and over to themselves (p. 382).

Students do need to be given proper materials, time, and patience to become familiar and comfortable while using phonics within the context of reading and writing. Children will express their knowledge of phonics when ready. If taught correctly combining the three-cueing systems (semantic, syntactic, and grapho-phonic), phonics will become part of students' daily reading and writing agenda.

Conclusion

This paper has presented some thorough and effective techniques for teaching phonics which engage students in gaining a knowledge and understanding of phonics for further success in their reading and writing experiences. Morrow and Tracey (1997) suggest that "teachers make a conscious effort to examine and reflect upon strategies they use for teaching phonics in order to select the best types of experiences for children to blossom effectively in the area of recognizing words and letters within the context of literature" (p. 651).

Throughout this paper, we as educators have learned that phonics, reading, and writing can occur simultaneously. Yes, phonics is necessary, but it must be taught within the context of a "meaning-filled" curriculum where students can use the three-cueing systems of semantics, syntax, and grapho-phonic cues. Students must also have various opportunities to construct their own meanings while reading, manipulating sounds, and writing their own words using various successful techniques along the way.

Educators need to join efforts to construct a universal curriculum where phonics will be successfully integrated within the context of quality literature. Students of all language backgrounds need to be immersed in phonics within a natural setting, so that they can easily transfer their skills within the context of written text. Most importantly, we as teachers need to be sensitive to students and their needs. At times these children will need direct assistance in phonics to enable them to break through any barriers in their reading progress, while some will advance successfully with indirect instruction.

Above all, we need to implement the techniques and insights these authors and experienced teachers have given us for further success in phonics within the context of meaningful life experiences. We as educators need to focus on responding to children's learning needs and to anticipate, not decide, what might be helpful to them in the future. Phonics will benefit students greatly any way it is taught. The question is, will they enjoy learning about phonics in every circumstance, and wil they be able to connect it to positive "real-life" experiences in the present and in their future?

References

Avery, C. (1993). *... And With A Light Touch.* Portsmouth, NH: Heinemann (A Division of Reed Elsevier, Inc.).

Hamers, J. F., and Blanc, M. H. A. (1989). *Bilinguality & Bilingualism.* NY: Press Syndicate of the University of Cambridge.

Krashen, S. D. (1988). Bilingual Education and Second Language Acquisition Theory. Office of Bilingual and Bicultural Education. *Schooling and Language Minority Students: A Theoretical Framework* (pp. 51-79). Los Angeles, CA: Evaluation, Dissemination and Assessment Center.

May, F. B. (1990). *Reading as Communication: An Interactive Approach.* Columbus, OH: Merrill Publishing Company.

Morrow, L. M., and Tracey, D. H. (1997). "Strategies Used for Phonics Instruction in Early Childhood Classrooms." *The Reading Teacher, 50,* (8), pp. 644-651.

Powell, D., and Hornsby, D. (1993). *Learning Phonics and Spelling in a Whole Language Classroom.* USA: Scholastic Inc.

Radencich, M. C. (1996). "Phonics and the Diverse Learner." In Harcourt Brace & Company, *Teaching Phonics : Staff Development Book.* USA: Harcourt Brace & Company, pp. 22-24.

_____. (1996). "Managing Phonics in the School Year and the School Day." In Harcourt Brace & Company, *Teaching Phonics: Staff Development Book.* USA: Harcourt Brace & Company, pp. 30-32.

Routman, R. (1994). *Invitations: Changing as Teachers and Learners K-12.* Portsmouth, NH: Heinemann (A Division of Reed Elsevier, Inc.).

Smith, P. (1996). "Phonics Instruction for the Nineties...and Beyond!" In *Teaching Phonics: Staff Development Book.* USA: Harcourt Brace & Company, pp. 13-15.

NOTES ON CONTRIBUTORS

BOBBIE ALLEN, PH.D. is a faculty member in the Teacher Education Program at the University of California, San Diego. She collaborated with other faculty members to develop an MA program in Teaching and Learning at UCSD that prepares teachers to implement ASL-English bilingual approaches with deaf children. Her research interest and publications have focused on ASL-English bilingual/bicultural classrooms for young deaf and hard of hearing children, effective bilingual teaching practices/approaches and the families' perspectives within these settings. She received a Ph.D. from the joint doctoral program--Claremont Graduate University and San Diego State University in May, 1998.

CAROLYN ANGUS is associate director of the George G. Stone Center for Children's Books of Claremont Graduate University. She is a frequent presenter of workshops for teachers, librarians, and parents. Her areas of special interest are children's literature and elementary science.

NANCY BRASHEAR is chair of the Teacher Education Department and Associate Professor of Education at Azusa Pacific University. She specializes in literacy development, children's literature, and reading.

LEILANI BROWN is a lecturer in Human Resources at the University of Hawaii where she specialized in teacher education, reading, and children's literature. She earned her B.A. and M.A. degrees at California State University Humboldt and completed her Ph.D. degree in education at Claremont Graduate University in 1989.

ALEJANDRO E. JAUREGUI received his BA from Biola University in Liberal Studies/Elementary Education in the spring of 1993. Currently, he is pursuing his MA in Education at the same institution and will complete his work in the fall of 1998. Alejandro has taught primary grades for five years and has focused on teaching multilingual students how to read and write in their primary as well as their secondary language. Teaching children is one of his true passions in life!

EVANGELINA BUSTAMANTE JONES, PH.D. is assistant professor in the department of Policy Studies in Language and Cross-Cultural Education, College of Education, San Diego State University. She received her Ph.D. in Education from the Joint Doctoral Program at Claremont Graduate University and San Diego State University. She has taught elementary and secondary grades, college writing courses, and now teaches in bilingual credential programs.

CLAIRE V. SIBOLD, PH.D., is a reading specialist with eight years teaching experience at the secondary level and 15 years of teaching experience at the university level. She is currently affiliated with Biola University (Education dept.) and earned her Ph.D. from Arizona State University.

FRANK SMITH is a writer and researcher living on Vancouver Island, British Columbia, Canada. He was born in England, took his undergraduate degree at the University of Western Australia, and has a Ph.D. in psycholinguistics from Harvard University. He has published short stories, poetry, a novel, and more than twenty books concerned with language and education. His most recent book is *The Book of Learning and Forgetting*, published by Teachers College Press in 1998.

STANLEY L. SWARTZ is professor of education at California State University, San Bernardino and lecturer in reading education at the University of California, Riverside. He was the director of Reading Recovery in California for many years and has been the director of California Early Literacy Learning since its inception. He is the editor of two Dominie Press series of little books for emergent readers, Carousel Readers and Teacher's Choice Series, and a skills development series for beginning readers, Building Blocks of Beginning Literacy. He is the editor of *Research in Reading Recovery,* recently published by Heinemann.

GAIL L. THOMPSON, PH.D., taught secondary school for 14 years. She is currently an assistant professor of Graduate Education at California State University, Dominguez Hills.

LIL THOMPSON has been a speaker at the Claremont Reading Conferences for over 25 years and always brings a special energy about

teaching and a love for young children which inspires and informs
everyone who has contact with her. Before her retirement she was
headmistress of a children's school in England, and she now resides in
Wolverhampton, West Midlands, England.

ROZANNE L. WILLIAMS (B.S. Education, Duquesne University) has
14 years experience as a classroom teacher, and has written over 100
books for emergent readers.

SHARON ZINKE is a resource specialist at Lorin Eden School in
Hayward, California. She has taught reading for over 30 years and was a
reading specialist for half of that time. She has provided staff
development for teachers and presentations for parents in the area of
literacy for the past 15 years. More recently, she has been active at the
state level fighting legislation which mandates a narrow view of research
in the area of reading.